MW00618678

To Muriel,
A good friend on
christmas 2003

Malcolm Lawrence

SOMETHING WILL COME ALONG

*Witty Memoirs of a Foreign Service
Officer with Nine Children*

SOMETHING WILL COME ALONG

*Witty Memoirs of a Foreign Service
Officer with Nine Children*

MALCOLM LAWRENCE

Publishing Group

www.ivyhousebooks.com

PUBLISHED BY IVY HOUSE PUBLISHING GROUP
5122 Bur Oak Circle, Raleigh, NC 27612
United States of America
919-782-0281
www.ivyhousebooks.com

ISBN: 1-57197-377-X
Library of Congress Control Number: 2003103965

Copyright © 2003 Malcolm Lawrence
All rights reserved, which includes the right to reproduce this book or por-
tions thereof in any form whatsoever except as provided by the U.S.
Copyright Law.

Printed in the United States of America

To my wife, Jacqueline

TABLE OF CONTENTS

INTRODUCTION

In 1937 when I was eleven years old and in the seventh grade, I met a pretty girl who was also eleven and in the seventh grade. She lived three blocks from me. Her name was Jacqueline. We went through school together. At age seventeen, we fell in love. After World War II we were married and had nine children.

On Labor Day in 1968, I called my children together and asked them to tell me their names, sex, and ages. This is what they said:

Theresa Ann	girl	21
Catherine	girl	20
Joan Marie	girl	18
Malcolm, Jr.	boy	17
Louise	girl	15
Joseph	boy	13
Frances	girl	10
Ann	girl	8
Ellen	girl	7

Jacqueline and I were 43 at the time. Intrigued by the answers, I asked more questions of our children and was amazed to learn that our family of eleven had a combined weight of 1,229 pounds. Our total age was 215 years. Stacked end-to-end in the air, we would have reached a height of 57 feet—imagine! The combined figure for weight, age, and height came to 1,501. Any way you looked at it, 1,501 was a lot.

Being personally responsible for a large portion of this number, I decided to trace the highlights and lowlights of my life and record how it all happened. My wife, who contributed quite a bit to the 1,501 herself, gave me much encouragement and served as an excellent memory jogger, for which I sincerely thank her.

For this, my first autobiography, I chose the fall of 1968 as a cut-off point to encompass those cherished and fleeting moments of family togetherness before the birds began departing the nest to embark upon lives of their own in the great world beyond.

Perhaps the Lawrence children will tell their own stories for the period after 1968. Some of my post-1968 activities are provided in Chapter Eleven and the four appendices.

★ *Chapter One* ★

PRELUDE

As any parent realizes, the truly formative years for children are from birth to thirteen. Yet when that parent looks back on his own youth, especially as he grows older, the formative years mysteriously shift to the range of thirteen to eighteen. True to this phenomenon, I can't remember much of importance that happened to me before age thirteen, but I'll think of something.

The record reveals that I was born on August 5, 1925 in Washington, D.C., the third child delivered unto my parents. My ancestral blood was a mixture of Spanish and English, but mine is one-hundred-percent American. My brother, sister, and I represent something like third-generation Washingtonians. Because of the transient nature of the Washington population, most people I come across express great disbelief that I—or anyone else for that matter—was born in that city. However, it makes for a good opening subject at cocktail parties.

During the Depression years, there were two things that didn't fail: the hunger of people in America and the United States government. The first had a lot to do with restoring the general economy, and the second guaranteed that the businesses in Washington, which were geared primarily to servicing the government, kept their heads fairly well out of water. My father, who was a banker, was able to maintain his payments for rent, automobile, refrigerator, and new superheterodyne radio, as well as to keep food on the table for us three, happy, inter-war period children. Thank God for peanut butter and jelly.

There were two things I do remember about my preschool days, and they both happened on the same day. When I was about three years old, I fell off my tricycle (after swerving to avoid running into a billy goat) and injured my knee. Some kind man picked me up and gave me a pinwheel, a toy that revolves when you blow on it. I really don't know why a man his age would have been carrying a pinwheel. That night, feeling very sorry for myself, but at the same time quite happy pinwheel-wise, I remember sitting in my highchair (I don't know why a kid my age was still in a highchair) and throwing buttered rice out of our fourth story window. If you think these two incidents lack interest, it is only because they didn't happen to you and on the same day yet.

The next thing I remember, I was in school and, like everybody else, received good grades. My big mistake was that along about fourth grade, I became particularly smart and skipped a half year. Naturally, the kids in my new class regarded me as a baby and hardly talked to me for weeks. However, I persevered and within five months was the youngest candidate for the schoolboy patrols. Needless to say, I made good and by the next term I was second lieutenant, directing traffic at one of the main corners. The following term, I was up for captain, but one of the first lieutenants, who quite naturally wanted the job himself, said I was too silly for the position. Mind you, not one life had been lost at my corner. The upshot was that both I and the overly ambitious first lieutenant lost, and the real clown of the school got the job. The accident rate at the new captain's corner was so high, the school had a traffic light installed to help out.

During the school seasons of my pre-adolescent days, our neighborhood gang—centered at First and Longfellow Streets, NW—enjoyed a wide variety of recreational activities. The popular games were hide and seek, kick the can, magic circle, red light, may I, and tag. We had special seasons for flip-cards, marbles, rubber-band guns, soap box cars (which we called jitney buses), roller skating, and skate-mobiles (made from two-by-fours and obsolete roller skates). In the spring, we built huts on vacant lots from materials we "acquired" from construction sites in that mushrooming section of Washington. When there was absolutely nothing else to do, we collected bottle tops, silver paper, or popsicle sticks. On rainy days, we played Monopoly.

Our favorite time was Halloween, and I shudder when I recall some of the things that went on in those days. As the practice of Trick or Treat was unknown to us, our poor victims didn't have a chance. Starting off at twilight, a gang of twenty to thirty of us roamed throughout a one-mile radius performing such dastardly deeds as ringing doorbells, soaping car and house windows, hanging fence gates and other movable items at the top of telephone poles, turning on outdoor water taps and throwing the knobs away, and tying opposite apartment door handles together. Some of the rougher gangs we observed used to shoot out streetlights, break windows, and place sewer tops against front doors. The most spectacular sight I witnessed on Halloween was when six boys carried an Austin car up a long flight of steps and deposited it on a front porch.

For four summers in a row, covering my tenth through thirteenth year, I was placed on a farm for my "vacation." This cost my parents about fifteen dollars a week and afforded me the opportunity of learning many worthwhile things—such as picking up stones and rocks from five hundred acres of fields in ninety-degree heat and throwing them into a horse-hitched wagon driven by the farmer's son, milking the cows, feeding the chickens, pitching hay, drowning kittens, chopping wood, tossing slop to pigs, making ice cream, skinning groundhogs, washing dishes, building fires, burying the garbage, and all the other things that most little boys simply love doing on vacations. On the odd occasion when I complained of fatigue, the farmer would jolly me up with his horsewhip until I regained my energy and went smilingly back to my holiday fun and games. The first three years I really didn't know the difference, but in the fourth year I wised up and toward the end of the summer season I shot the farmer in the seat with a popgun. He hardly felt it, but I was scared and ran away. I walked twenty-three miles before a kind man (not the one with the pinwheel) picked me up and drove me the rest of the way to Washington, D.C.

At age eleven, I had graduated from J. R. Keene Elementary School at Blair and Riggs Roads, NE, and volunteered to attend Paul Junior High at 8th and Oglethorpe Streets, NW. I really can't remember what the schoolwork was like, but I did begin to notice that girls were somewhat different from boys—their voices were higher pitched. I was lousy at baseball, so I joined the track and tumbling teams. I became the second-fastest runner in school, primarily to keep away from the third-fastest boy, who was a bully. Also, before long I was the star tumbling expert and used to perform occasionally on the stage during school assemblies, bashing my head on the mats in a series of head-and-hand flips. To this day, I don't know what it proved, but I was told it would help me later in life.

From my twelfth year on, I began to get industrious. My father drank only so much ginger ale and assorted soft drinks, and I found it difficult to keep myself in spending money by cashing in the bottles for pennies at the store. So I set myself up in a number of interesting and lucrative jobs. I got a morning paper route, for which I earned about three dollars a week. On Thursday and Friday evenings, I delivered prescriptions and other items on bicycle for the local drugstore (earning about one dollar per night). On Saturdays, I delivered groceries by wagon and stocked shelves at the local supermarket (making two and a half dollars on a good day). At some point or another, I took on an afternoon job of selling *Liberty Magazine* and *Country Gentleman* door-to-door. I occasionally distributed the local *Shopping News* and handed out sample breakfast foods and soap packages. Whatever my jobs, I never missed the radio broadcasts of "Little Orphan Annie" (primarily to work out the messages on my decoder pins), and of "Ma Perkins" (to send away for flower seeds to give to my mother). Then there were "Jack Armstrong," "Vic and Sade," and "Tom Mix."

Shortly thereafter (it must have been when I was thirteen because I didn't send away for my 1939 decoder pin, and didn't care), I began to take an interest in music. I listened to Tommy Dorsey, Benny Goodman, Artie Shaw, Larry Clinton, Count Basie, Duke Ellington, and Charlie Barnet. I fell in love with the sound of the tenor saxophone and yearned to play it. In those days I used to provide rhythmic accompaniment to the radio broadcasts and records of the big bands on assorted pots, pans, and dishes, singing along in unison with the saxophone solos. I thought I was pretty good, but hardly anyone else shared my tolerance for noise. At any rate, in my fourteenth year, I walked into a downtown music store with the intention of signing up for saxophone lessons. A beautiful, pearl-finish drum set was on display. I marched over, touched it, and signed up for fifty-two drum lessons instead.

My instructor was not a drummer at all, but a trombone player. Not knowing I was left-handed, he started me out as a right-handed drummer. Technically, only another drummer would understand the difference. So for my non-drummer readers I shall explain. A left-handed drummer should normally hold his sticks just the reverse of a right-handed drummer. My drummer readers might not agree, but most right-handed drummers who hold the sticks right-handed invariably end up with a weak left hand, which hangs somewhere above the snare drum while the naturally stronger right hand, which is employed to hit everything but the kitchen sink, does most of the work. You non-drummers can readily understand that by forcing my weak hand (the right) to develop a striking technique for the various things a drummer must hit with the right hand (cymbals, tom-toms, cow bells, etc.), I was able to equalize the versatility and speed of both hands. All left-handed non-drummers may have a ten-minute break for practice.

Practice was my motto and with it plenty of noise. We lived in a row house at the time, and my neighbors for blocks around clearly loathed me, especially in the summer months when I played with the windows open. In the beginning, they simply had no ear for music; in the end they had no ear at all.

Having dispensed and dispersed rhythmic torture for a year, I began to develop a little finesse and joined my first dance band at age fifteen, playing high school proms, country clubs, firemen's carnivals, and tea dances. In keeping with the hip fashion of the day, I wore a zoot suit, an outfit featuring a long jacket and pegged trousers, and my hair was quite thick. I linked up with a bigger and better band several months later, graduating to college dances, roadhouses, and hotel ballrooms. I got a haircut, bought a new suit, joined the musician's union at age seventeen, and folded into a much smaller combo which played strictly on the hotel circuit; it was less dynamic, but paid better than non-union jobs.

To play drums in a dance band, you have to love your drum set and put it together in a most precise way—the way it suits you personally. No two drummers do it alike, but there are some basic things that all drummers do. Let's look at the bass drum first; you apply spurs to the bottom rims, front and back, to keep it from rolling and sliding. Then, attach the foot pedal, which makes the sound, and mufflers to deaden the noise. Next, affix the tom-toms, cymbal holders, and cymbals. The snare drum, which has a stand of its own, does most of the work and has to be set at the usual exact height and tilt. The drummer's throne (seat) comes next; if it is too high or low, your performance will not be your best. Then, set up the "hi-hat," the standing assembly that permits you to open and close two matching cymbals with your left foot. Finally, you tune all of the drum heads to achieve the sounds you desire. When all of this is accomplished, you are ready for the job and you sit on your throne poised in suspense waiting for the band leader to beat off the tempo for the opening tune. There is no thrill in life quite like it.

I shift now to a different kind of thrill. It was my dabbling in music that indirectly led to my dating Jackie. We had, as I indicated, known each other from the seventh grade on. I had always thought she was sort of cute for a girl, but there had been nothing in particular to draw us together. She hung around with a bunch of friends who seemed to be interested in little other than getting good grades.

During our junior high school years, we nodded a couple of times at one another. But when we were in the tenth grade at Coolidge High School, Fifth and Tuckerman Streets, NW, I took a much closer look and saw that she had beautiful brown eyes, attractive auburn hair, and a graceful, well-appointed figure— about five-foot-four and 110 pounds, I guessed. It was shortly after that when she started kicking my hallway locker shut and twisting the three-way combination dial after I had just struggled to open the thing. For revenge, I used to call her "Sweater Girl," which always seemed to bring a crimson color to her cheeks. I assumed at the time that she must have had high blood pressure or something.

But back to the music tie-in. One morning in the spring of 1942 (twelfth grade), I brought to school about a dozen glossy photographs of myself in various poses whacking away at the drums. They had been taken by a school chum of mine who was an excellent amateur photographer. During a study period that morning, I circulated the photos in the class, not to show everybody how scintillating I looked on drums, but to exhibit the fine photographic talents of my friend. At the end of the period, I announced that if everyone had finished examining the outstanding photographs, I would appreciate having the pictures returned. There was no response. The bell rang, and everyone got up and left the room. Dirty work was afoot. I asked another one of my friends (I had more than one, you know) if he had any knowledge as to the whereabouts of the photos. He replied that he had seen Jackie Drullard slip them into her notebook just before the bell rang.

It was difficult to figure whether she was having her revenge for my Sweater Girl comment or just hadn't had time to examine the fine points of the photography before class ended. There was also another explanation, which was the correct one, but it didn't occur to me until I asked her a week later to return the photos. She turned that damned crimson color again. I knew then, without letting on, that she didn't have high blood pressure. After that, my thoughts wandered more and more in her direction. But I was an independent cuss, and there were always those smart friends of hers. I contained my emotions, threw myself into my schoolwork, and went on beating the drums until the end of the semester.

On June 14, 1942, I was calmly spending Sunday morning washing my brother-in-law's car in front of my house. While I was scrubbing the rear outside wheel, I was frightened almost to death by an oncoming car swerving in my direction and blaring its horn. Behind the wheel was Jackie, laughing her crimson head off. As she went by, she stuck out her tongue, which as I recall was also red. From my frozen position, I jumped into "my" car, a 1942 convertible Buick, and followed in hot pursuit. It didn't take me long to catch her, as she lived just up the street and around the corner. I pulled behind her father's car, a '41 Chevy with a white base and a red top, jumped out of my brother-in-law's car, and led myself "down the garden path." Jackie said "Hi" and ran into the house to fix a gallon of lemonade. From then on we went steady. We were voted the "cutest couple" of the senior class and graduated from high school in February 1943.

Jackie's father had been sick for a year (he passed away the following April), and she went to work with the Navy Department to help support the family and the war effort. I started school at the George Washington University. I took a number of interesting subjects, but what I remember most was that I fancied myself as some kind of a boxer. Being left-handed (here we go again), I was trained to move to the right and beat my right-handed adversaries to the punch with my right jab. After having jabbed their left eyes to the closed position in two or three rounds, I would then swing a low, looping left into their proverbial breadbaskets and emerge victorious. It was a fairly simple formula which stood me in good stead until I reached the finals of the end-of-season tournament, when I discovered at the last moment that my opponent was also left-handed. He had apparently boxed against left-handers before and knew what to do. I hadn't and didn't. In round one, my left eye was closed, in two I was eliminated on a TKO. From that night, I decided to give up boxing. I was to do a little more of it later, however, as I shall relate in due course.

By age eighteen, I had finished one semester of college, gone steady with Jackie for a year, worked two summers with the

Washington Gas-Light Company (first as a messenger and then as an office-machine operator), and become the best drummer in Washington (primarily because all of the other drummers had been drafted). I was ready for manhood and bigger and better things.

★ *Chapter Two* ★

WINNING THE WAR

Like many others, I was invited by my local draft board to help win World War II. I reported to the Induction Center on October 25, 1943. Traveling is broadening, but that was ridiculous. In two years and thirty-nine days in the Air Force, I was sent to the following places:

Camp Lee, Virginia—Induction center
Fort George Meade, Maryland—Placement center
Miami Beach, Florida—Basic training center
Sioux Falls, South Dakota—Radio school
Yuma, Arizona—Gunnery school
Washington, D.C.—Furlough
Tampa, Florida—Processing center
Gulfport, Mississippi—Flight training center
Fort Dix, New York—Flight demonstration assignment
Savannah, Georgia—Staging area

Manchester, New Hampshire—Port of embarkation

Goose Bay, Labrador—Overseas departure outpost

Belfast, Northern Ireland—Arrival center

Valley, Wales—Processing center

Stone, England—Assignment center

Bury St. Edmunds, England—Base of operations

Secret location, England—Rest Home

Chorley, England—Replacement depot

Stone, England—Redeployment depot

Tidworth, England—Port of embarkation

Brooklyn, New York—Return staging area

Fort George Meade, Maryland—Discharge center

I was no oddball. These were, in fact, the places one had to go to be a Radio Operator Gunner on a B-17 bomber and conclude a tour of missions over Europe, which is what I did.

Of course I wanted to be an officer, but I didn't make it. At Fort Meade, I had passed the exams for both Officers' Candidate School and Air Cadet Training and chose the latter. Several weeks later at Miami Beach, our class of five hundred was "washed out" because the Air Force already had too many pilots, navigators, and bombardiers. It was naturally our consensus that all who made officer before us were morons and illiterates. This wasn't entirely true, but it made us feel better.

My favorite place was, nevertheless, Miami Beach, where I received basic training. We stayed at the Blackstone Hotel, and the roughest part of all was getting to and from my room, which was on the eleventh floor (we couldn't use the elevators). We swam every morning in the ocean and had calisthenics before breakfast. The rest of the time we had close-order drill and listened to lectures and watched films on venereal diseases. (It seemed somewhat implausible, if not impossible, that every place

I was stationed during the war had the highest rate of VD in the world. Either all but one of the Air Force doctors were lying or the guy spreading it was in my outfit.) In my spare time, I played with a seventeen-piece Air Force dance band at the First Street Pier—four trumpets, four trombones, five saxes, and a four-piece rhythm section. Everyone blasted so loud, I couldn't even hear my own "instrument." That is always seventh heaven for a drummer.

Next to being an officer, my "second choice" was to be an enlisted man. I was sent to Air Force radio school at Sioux Falls, where the temperature on arrival was two degrees above zero, compared with a nice seventy-two at Miami Beach. Radio school was six months of taking radio receivers and transmitters apart, putting them together again, and learning to send and receive Morse code.

One day while there, I wandered into the gym and saw a few fellows with boxing gloves on. They were punching bags and each other. Nostalgia overtook me. I slipped into some twelve-ounce gloves and puttered around for a while on the speed and punching bags. Then I looked for someone to joust with. I spotted a hotshot character and asked him if he wanted to spar for a couple of rounds. He said, "Sure, buddy," so we got into the ring. As in the old days, I poked my right into his left eye and thought he was going to be a pushover. It went that way for three rounds. At the propitious moment, I swung my devastating, long-looping left toward his belly and was knocked out. When I recovered, I discovered that my opponent had been Billy Conn's sparring partner prior to Conn's match with Joe Louis in 1941 when Conn had almost beaten the "Brown Bomber." I put two and two together and decided that I didn't want to be the heavyweight champion of the world. However, I assumed that Conn would quickly defeat Louis in the return match after the war, which in itself would place me within the top ten heavyweight contenders.

My base of operations for the bombing missions was the 94th Bomb Group of the 8th Air Force at Bury St. Edmunds, England. A typical day started early. A gentle awakening at 3:15 A.M. was followed by a dash to the latrine along with sixty other airmen to wash hands and face, then back to the hut for complete dressing, after which a mad run ensued for the mess hall on bicycle over a winding dirt path through one mile of woods in pitch darkness. (As one couldn't use lights, one had to learn this path by heart. During the course of a month, one crew member smashed head-on into trees four times and cycled off a ten-foot cliff.) Next, a hearty breakfast of fried eggs and coffee took place (on non-mission days, we had powdered eggs, which provided our greatest incentive for flying even dangerous missions). At 4:10 A.M. a briefing on the mission took place, and take-off at 5:50 A.M. led to a six- to ten-hour mission, depending on the target location. Then we would return to base, unload, clean guns, and proceed to interrogation, where each crew member was given a double shot of cognac (two of our crew didn't drink, so a couple of others had quadruple shots—ugh). From there, we went back to the hut to wash up and try before dark (for obvious reasons) to cycle up to and back from the mess hall.

Some time between 6:00 and 7:00 P.M., we returned to the hut to rest our weary heads. Then a caller stuck his head in the door and announced that tomorrow would be another beautiful day, and a 3:00 A.M. flight call was in order. In our exhausted state, the prospect of having to do anything was truly demoralizing. On the other hand, when our little announcer indicated bad weather for two days, all of us leaped from bed to apply for passes to London. Actually, I went to London eleven times in six months, but didn't see much because of fog and blackout conditions, despite which I still managed to acquire a "feel" for the city.

For a little flavor, I reproduce below the notes I made on mission No. 17 on April 8, 1945. Target: Plauen, Germany.

It's 7:30 A.M., and we're at five thousand feet. Never have I seen such a beautiful sunrise. The solid white clouds lie just as even as water.

Here comes the sun peeping out of the east. In the distance I can see tiny white and black specks: heavy bombers forming for today's mission.

Our ship, which is just behind the lead, is surrounded by planes of our group. The tails of our planes are yellow with the letter A in a white square.

The sun is a little higher now, making the clouds more beautiful than before. On the left, a quarter moon is barely visible. Nothing but clear sky above the sea of clouds.

If only I could step out and walk on the surface of these clouds. It looks possible—even easy.

A flock of B-24s is now passing over our formation. The lead plane is dropping the usual flares for recognition. About seventy or eighty other ships are following him.

Well, we crossed the English Channel and are now over Belgium. Little towns and communities are spaced here and there. Seems as though we left the clouds over England because there isn't a trace of them here. Even though we're at six thousand feet, I can still make out some of the particulars below.

10:30: Below is the Moselle River—many extreme turns—resembles a huge snake.

10:45: Entered enemy territory. Passing over some fairly large cities. We're now at eleven thousand feet and climbing to fifteen thousand, which is our bombing altitude. If the weather is this good at the target, we can't possibly miss.

On the bomb run, which is about ten to fifteen minutes before the target, I began throwing chaff.

12:40: Dropped the bombs—pretty good too. Just as I was checking to see if all the bombs had been released from our ship, a huge burst of flak under the bomb-bay section shook the whole ship.

12:50: Well, I'll be damned! The rest of the bomb groups have gone back toward Belgium and our ships are circling around over Germany. From what I've heard, the jet-jobs like to attack lone formations—sure hope they don't get any ideas.

That's not the only reason I'm griping. If we hang around much longer, there might not be any cocoa and sandwiches in the briefing room—forget the cognac. The ones that land first hog all the food. Oh well, worse things could happen.

Apparently, some of the ships in our group didn't drop all of their bombs, and there was talk of the group making a second run over the target. But it didn't happen.

A batch of P-51s, our fighter escort, circled our group and helped us depart enemy territory. Those guys fly as if they owned the sky—and they do.

3:00: Now we're over the Channel. Should be landing in about forty minutes.

Land ho! At this time I shall rid myself of my flying clothes and stuff them in the barracks bag, so I won't have to waste so much time in the locker room. Just have to get to those refreshments.

Not a bad landing. Signing off, Malcolm Lawrence, R.O.G., Crew 35

The most vivid memory of my tour of duty is a brief but poignant incident occurring at midday on March 18, 1945. Our crew was approaching the target over Berlin on the largest daylight raid of the war. In my April 8 notes, I mentioned "chaff." During bomb runs, as a radio-operator-gunner, it was my job on instruction from the co-pilot to release packages of tin-foil strips, known as "window" or "chaff" through a chute behind the radio operator's swivel seat. The purpose of this operation was to throw off radar-controlled, anti-aircraft guns by creating a blur on the sights instead of a precise target.

On the March 18 Berlin bomb run, five hundred batteries of German guns were filling the air with exploding flak. The co-pilot said on intercom, "Co-pilot to radio, start tossing chaff." Just as I turned to commence releasing tin-foil, a piece of flak tore a three-inch hole through the left side of the plane—chest high—at the very spot I had been sitting one second earlier. The flak passed through the right side of the plane, making a much bigger hole.

That was quite a scare for a nineteen-year-old. Such a shot in my side would have ripped me asunder. Needless to say, I thanked the co-pilot for his timely command. During our twenty-three missions, we flew through all kinds of flak and were challenged by German jets. We lost engines, had two forced landings and experienced other dangers. But that piece of flak on mission number eight over Berlin had my name on it. I thank God that I am able to write about it.

My radio training really came in handy on one of our missions. After dropping our bombs over Germany, we were headed back to base when storm conditions and darkness threw us off course. The pilot was flying blind for almost an hour. The navigator reckoned we were out somewhere over the North Sea, but he could not determine our position. The crew was tense. I sent messages in Morse code to three radio stations and received "fixes." Where the three lines intersected gave me the geographic location of our plane. I passed the coordinates on to the pilot, who set the course for home. We made it back safely with very little fuel to spare. It had been pretty scary. The crew was most relieved that we did not have to ditch the plane in the freezing North Sea.

The nice thing about flying combat missions, as opposed to being in the infantry, was that life was fairly normal between flights. Unlike our ground-based brethren who were in constant danger, we were exposed only while flying over enemy territory. Consequently, after a tour of missions, our crew was certainly not shell-shocked and, in fact, felt pretty good about life in general. However, we were told we had been under a tremendous strain. And so it was in late April 1945 that we were sent to a "rest home" for ten days, a beautiful English villa. There were eight attractive hostesses living there to help us recuperate. Among other games, we played tennis, volleyball, and craps. The local village was gifted with no less than thirteen pubs. I was completely exhausted after the ten days and still wonder why it was called a rest home.

While our crew was there, the war had virtually ended in Europe. I was in London on V-E Day, May 8, watching the movie "The Picture of Dorian Gray," featuring Hurd Hatfield, George Sanders and Angela Lansbury. In the middle of the film, an announcement on the public address system proclaimed that the war in Europe was officially over. Hundreds of us rushed out of the theater into Piccadilly Circus and witnessed the wildest celebration known to man, woman or beast. Thousands of people had filled the area, and some eager beavers were even climbing up the statue of Eros, the Greek god of love. That was a most appropriate spot because girls young and old were chasing and hugging and kissing every military man on the scene. It was a miracle that I managed to escape—after about an hour. Incidentally, the manager had told us we could come back to watch the end of the movie, which many of us did at no extra charge.

For a number of reasons, it took from May to November to redeploy us to the States. Perhaps the most significant explanation was that our navigator fell ill. We lost the plane to another crew and were unable to fly home. For redeployment purposes, we had to compete with members of the infantry and other ground forces from the continent, who had anywhere from one hundred to two hundred "points." Being relatively short-term fly-boys, we had much less, around seventy to eighty of the go-home credits, so we had to sweat it out.

For most of the period, we stayed at a "reple-deple" (replacement depot) at Chorley, where living took on the truest form of democracy. That is, we had to wait on each other. Combat-hardened tech sergeants and master sergeants found themselves lining up every morning and taking orders and daily work assignments from a "permanent-party" corporal who proudly wore ribbons for the American and European Theaters of Operation, the Good Conduct medal, and a sharpshooter award. Moreover, his spit-shined boots were a sight for all to behold. After a succession of crummy daily jobs, I, even though only a lowly staff sergeant, was assigned as a semi-permanent "block chief," a title which gave me the privilege of performing the full range of duties as a barracks janitor. I pulled an inspection twice a week and took great pleasure in telling the two master sergeants in my charge that unless they kept their bunk areas neater I would report them to the corporal.

Things got so bad during that period I even took to writing poetry, to wit:

The Forlorn Soldier
Here I sit overseas.
All I ask is one boat please.
And let me stow away upon it,
Lest I have a royal fit.

I miss my girl, I miss my home,
I miss a chocolate ice cream cone,
Though home and cone do not rhyme,
I'll consider that some other time.

I long to ride in automobiles
And wear heel-plates on my heels.
But most of all I'd like to scrutinize
My gal-friend's rootin'-tootin' eyes.

Here's hoping that my wish comes true
And that it doesn't go askew.
My unhappiness would surely end
If some kind soul would condescend and kinda send
ME HOME.

I wrote that on October 27, 1945 and sent it to Jackie. She told me sometime later that it touched her heart and wondered if I had joined the Ogden Nash School of Poetry.

One day during this period of waiting to go home, a friend of mine named Waggy and I went to a carnival in Chorley. One of the features there was a boxer who was willing to take on all comers. Two pounds sterling (eight dollars and six cents in those days) would be awarded to an opponent for each round he could remain on his feet against the Terrible Tiger. The guy was at least thirty years old and must have weighed 240 pounds. I was standing about fifteen yards from ringside watching the character batter the daylights out of some poor joker. There was a thud. A defeated amateur crawled out of the ring. Waggy, who had heard all about my prowess as a boxer (because I had told him), went up to talk to the manager and pointed me out in the crowd. Both the manager and the Terrible Tiger looked out at me as I raised my 178 pounds on tiptoes to see what was going on. Waggy came back and said the Tiger had been afraid to take me on. "I told them you were Billy Conn," he said. "Small wonder," I commented, feeling considerably calmer than before. Later that night in a pub, Waggy got into a fight at the bar with two British soldiers while I sipped my beer at a table. Everyone simmered down, and Waggy came back to the table. "What happened?" I asked. "It was all because they had never heard of Billy Conn," he told me. We carried each other back to the base. I felt confident I could lick Joe Louis after the war.

At long last, I sailed home on the SS *Europa*, a former German luxury liner converted to a troop ship. This trip it "accommodated" some nine thousand GIs. The bunks were piled six-high everywhere. I slept on the fifth tier in the dining room and fell out only once. The principal activity on the cruise was eating; we waited in chow lines a full seven hours out of our waking day. After docking in New York and spending a week in Brooklyn, we were sent by rail to Fort Meade, Maryland. On my final day in the Air Force, I and a large number of other overly-anxious youths were asked to turn in all of our GI issue clothing (except for one full uniform to wear home). I threw one tan sock and a dirty, torn tee-shirt onto the conveyor belt, picked up my B-4 bag, and ran out into the free, fresh-smelling postwar world.

★ *Chapter Three* ★

COLLEGE DAYS PLUS TAX

Having won the war practically singlehandedly, with a little help from sixteen million other GIs, I decided to have a try at civilian life. What to do? During my stint in the service, I had dreamed of many things I wanted to be: a professional drummer (maybe), an airline pilot (to prove to the world that I could fly), an insurance salesman (to make a quick killing), a banker (but then my father was one of these), a college student (never), a professional drummer (I kept coming back to it), a radio-operator-gunner in a heavy bomber (there wouldn't be much demand for it in peace-time), an ideas man (this sounded like a good start), a husband (ye gods!), a professional drummer . . . (why not?).

In any event, when I was honorably discharged from the Air Force on December 2, 1945, I didn't know what I wanted to do. First of all, I went over to Jackie's place on Madison Street in Washington, gave her a kiss on the cheek, said "Hello" and asked her if she had anything in the house to eat. She fixed me a meal and asked me what I was going to do now that the war was over.

I told her I was going to relax for a few days and think it over. I gave her another kiss on the cheek and left.

I went home and thought for a couple of days. On the third day, I received a telephone call from Stan Brown, my premilitary-days orchestra leader, who inquired whether I would be interested in returning to music. I said yes. In fact, I told him I was seriously considering becoming a full-time musician and eventually hitting the big time. He coughed and said all he could offer was a few nights a week as before. He related as to how music, at least live music, was on the wane and that with the return of all the musicians from the war, it would behoove me to accept his offer and return to the schmaltzy brand of noise (the two-beat, the waltz, the soppy ballad, and the prewar rendition of "Saints"). I said I'd let him know in a few days.

I went back to Jackie's the next Sunday, gave her another kiss on the cheek, and said that I was going back into the music business. She told me it would ruin her Christmas. When I said I didn't understand, she pulled a package out of the closet (which she always called the cupboard) and told me to open my Christmas present early. I did. It was a thirty-nine-dollar, genuine leather bookbag, complete with three dividers, two straps, a handle, and a brass lock. She said simply, "I wanted you to go back to college." Tears fell from her eyes (where else?) and she looked sheepishly to the floor. What could I do? I said I would investigate whether the university would take me back after all this time.

So the next day I went down to the registrar's office of the George Washington University and told a young female clerk that years ago I had gone to the school and asked if there would be any chance of my returning. She told me that there were 13,000 World War II veterans applying for the spring term and to sit down. I sat in a waiting room containing not quite 13,000 ex-GIs, but almost. I noticed that very few of them had turned in much of their army clothing upon discharge (which was, of course, mandatory). In an attempt to be different, I pulled the collar of my Eisenhower dress battle jacket up to cover my olive drab shirt from view. I couldn't do much about my paratrooper boots, however. So I guess they all figured I was an ex-supply sergeant.

About an hour later, the same girl called me over to the counter and said she had located my records. I had a 2.6 average, not counting physical education. I told her I knew I had flunked out in my studies, but hoped that my excellent boxing record at the school would have pulled me through. I explained to her about my famous fight there with the left-hander. She said something about my being a Section Eight and told me to stop poking my right fist in her face. Then she informed me that a 2.6 average was not failing and that inasmuch as I had attended the university previously, I could come back in a month and register for the spring term with a good chance of being accepted. I was also told that I didn't have to take boxing anymore as I was a veteran. About the boxing I felt good—about going to school again, not so sure. Anyway, I told her I would be back in four weeks, went into the waiting room, slipped into my Air Force overcoat, and threw a snappy salute to all the ex-GIs. All returned the salute expertly and one, in doing so, dropped his mess kit on the floor. "C'est la guerre," I commented as I marched out of the swinging doors into two equally swinging co-eds.

I dashed to Jackie's house on the streetcar (which wasn't easy), rang her doorbell, but it was broken, so I knocked. After a few minutes, she answered. Her hair was half up in curlers. I told her I had practically been accepted at the university. She went into another room and returned with her auburn hair spilling loosely around her shoulders. This time, she kissed me on the cheek (not quite).

She gasped, "Now we can get . . . "

"Hush," I quieted her. "Don't talk at a moment like this."

After having some grilled cheese sandwiches, I went home. I was living in Arlington, Virginia at the time with my mother and father. I telephoned my pre-military orchestra leader and said, "Stan, I've decided to postpone being a big time musician for a while and rejoin your group instead." Stan was so delighted, he had another coughing attack. Shortly thereafter, I located a part-time afternoon job at the Veterans Administration (where else?), started classes at GW, and began playing two or three nights a week in the band, mostly at the Statler Hotel.

With part of my mustering-out pay, I bought a 1937 twelve-cylinder Lincoln Zephyr, just like the Green Hornet's, except it was canary-yellow instead of black. It looked super and only had eighty-five thousand miles on it. However, I was soon to learn that it ate up almost as much oil as gasoline, which was considerable because it only did something like seven miles to the gallon. The frustrations involved in getting it from one gas station to another began to affect my scholastic activities and make serious inroads on my mental stability, so I had to sell it. I had installed a second-hand radio. As there was no on-off switch, I had hooked it up directly to the ignition. Two weeks after I sold the car, some man telephoned me and inquired, "How in the name of hell do you turn off the radio?" Of all the questions.

I proposed to Jackie, bought her an engagement ring (with the money I got from the car), and we were married shortly thereafter. We had a fairly large formal wedding (to which my mother was twenty-five minutes late) and settled down to married life. This was quite a step for Jackie, who gave up her own prospective career to help put me through school. She had been attending the University of Maryland, majoring in English and minoring in the humanities. She had planned either to teach high school in the States or educate half of the population of South America.

After a riotous, fun-filled honeymoon in New York, we moved into our first home at Thirteenth and Clifton Streets, NW. We had a one-room efficiency apartment with a hide-away bed. We cooked on a hotplate, one side of which was always breaking down, ate on a card table, and washed clothes in the bathtub. When company knocked at the door, we simply lifted up the bed, jammed it into an already filled all-purpose closet (which Jackie called the cupboard), and slid an easy chair into the spot vacated by the bed. We would then open the door and let in our guests. "What a lovely apartment," they usually said. "Where is the bedroom?" We would point to the closet door and say, "Oh, in through there."

Another nice feature: our place was full of roaches. After several months of slamming the poor devils to death, we discovered that ours was the only apartment not benefiting from the weekly spraying service. It turned out that we had every roach in the building, but were too shy and embarrassed to mention our problem to the resident manageress. I had even sneaked roach-infested pieces of furniture out at midnight and deposited them on a vacant lot. One of our neighbors tipped us off about the spraying service, and life became easier in that respect.

We had other problems though, particularly money. Our basic income was my subsistence allowance under the GI Bill of Rights. This was supplemented by my earnings from the band and my part-time work at the Veterans Administration. However, it was barely sufficient to keep us in peanut butter and corn flakes, much less provide a nest egg for a house. So, Jackie began working full-time at the telephone company.

On a typical work day, we arose at 7:00 A.M. had breakfast, and departed together by streetcar. We put in our respective efforts and reached home about 6:00 P.M. While she set the card table and tinkered around with the tempermental hotplate, I went to the grocery store and selected the evening meal. Our "dining room" was in a narrow hallway just inside the entrance. In fact, one could hardly enter or leave the apartment while the table was set. A compensating factor, however, was that we usually had dinner by candlelight. We could barely see what we were eating, but being romantic newlyweds, we really didn't much care. After the meal, I gallantly drew water from the bathtub faucet, placed the pan on the card table, and thereby automatically converted the dining room into our "kitchen." While Jackie did the dishes, I set about doing my homework at a giant eighty-year-old desk which took up at least half of the apartment. After two or three quiet hours of studying and reading, we would swing the hide-away bed down, change into our night garments, and snuggle down to slumberland.

Our peace was invariably interrupted, however, by the collapse of the bed to the floor. Despite all attempts, I couldn't keep that damned thing from buckling. I dare say the bed agitated our neighbors below as much as it did us. In any event, once it collapsed, we just left it that way until morning. We got pretty sick of it after three or four months, and I almost complained to the resident manageress, but I didn't want her to think that in addition to being the only couple with a roach problem, we had problems in bed.

I enjoyed my classes very much, especially the history class of 1,300 students in Lisner auditorium. Talk about individual attention; from the twelfth row in the balcony, I could hardly see what the professor looked like. Most of us up there failed the first two tests because we didn't know they were being given. The professor finally started using a microphone, and we learned that he had a most pleasant and informative voice, indeed. The teacher/student ratio was slightly better in the other classes, but I had great doubts during my first three semesters whether my teachers had any idea who I was.

The grind of my studies was interrupted one evening when Jackie said, "Malc, I have a funny feeling in my stomach."

"No small wonder with that meal we had."

"But it's different this time," she replied. "I think we're going to have . . . "

"Have what?" I gasped.

"I think that soon we will be three."

"Would that it be true, but I still think it is the roundsteak. Get thee to a doctor, go."

"Oh, Malc, won't it be wonderful?"

"Of course," I replied quietly. I was studying Malthus at the time and was well on my way to becoming a neo-Malthusian. Secretly, however, I was tickled pink at the prospect of having a fine son, a true carbon copy of myself. Another great boxer perhaps. But then I recalled that Billy Conn had failed miserably in his postwar re-match with Louis.

The baby was born on June 7, 1947. I went to see Jackie that day after my 9:00 A.M. class and said, "I fell down the steps this morning and hurt my elbow."

"That's too bad," she said. "What do you think of the baby?"

"Oh, I think it's fine. Girls are nice."

For four days during my visits to the hospital, we talked about a name for the child. On the fifth day, a nurse came into the room and said she must have a name for the records immediately. Jackie put the name "Theresa" up to a vote. We all agreed. "Make that Theresa Ann," Jackie said and fell asleep, contented with the thought that her first born would not, after all, end up with the name "Baby Lawrence."

We discovered that the crowded little apartment could become even more crowded. We bought everything a baby needs, ordered diaper service, and learned how to prepare that feast of feasts—the formula.

The following November, when Theresa was barely five months old, I came home with the news that the part-time work program at the Veterans Administration was being discontinued as of December 1. This, plus the loss of Jackie's income, certainly didn't promise a very merry Christmas. I managed to locate a job for the holidays as a temporary mail carrier in the Friendship Heights area of Washington. I couldn't afford a pair of warm shoes and damned near got frostbite, but the money helped.

We didn't have many presents that year, but we certainly had a large tree which practically took up the other half of the apartment. My father, who always made a point of visiting his children on Christmas day with his 8-mm movie camera, spent about two hours at our place, but the best he could come up with under the circumstances was a bunch of close-up shots of our little family peering out from between the tree and the writing desk. The hotplate came through like crazy, and Jackie was able to prepare a nice roast in the new pressure cooker we gave each other.

On New Year's Eve, Jackie accompanied me on the band job. She wasn't exactly happy to go to these things because they made her feel like an orchestra wife. I reminded her what a thrill it was to sit there and watch me play drums for hours without being bothered by other men. At times, I really believed she was narrow-minded.

One day in mid-January, I dashed into the apartment and shook my college grades in Jackie's face. "Look. A 3.2 average, and I have only one more semester to go before my BA degree."

"Malc?" she replied.

"Wait! Let me finish; that isn't all. I found a new part-time job as an Engineering Aid in the Radio Control Section of the Trimetrogon Division of the Geological Survey in the Department of the Interior. I'll be working with maps, charts, and aerial photography flights, tying successive pictures of a flight together through common terrain detail and linking parallel or converging flights together through detail on the inside wing pictures of the flights concerned . . . "

"Malc?"

"And I'll be making azimuth transfers where flights cross or touch and correcting for tip and tilt of the planes which took the photographs. Moreover, I'll be plotting control stations on maps and on overlay sheets for maps and. . . "

"That is nice, Malc," she said. "Malc?"

"What?"

"I have a funny feeling in my stomach."

"Of course you do," I shot back. "In just four months' time, I shall graduate. I can get a full-time professional job and then . . . "

"It's not that," she whispered. "I think we're going to be four."

"That's wonderful," I said, collapsing on the collapsed hideaway bed.

Early in February, I started my new job and a new term at school. The part-time music career continued as a necessary evil. In March, when Jackie began to show, I went to the resident manageress and explained that my wife was with child and that it would be a little crowded with four people in one room. She surprised me by announcing that a larger apartment would become vacant within a month. I broke the news to Jackie and dashed out to buy a bottle of wine.

We moved into the new apartment in April. To us, it was cavernous. Although there was only one bedroom, it was huge, and we had a real living room, a real dining room, an honest-to-goodness kitchen and even a small screened porch to air baby Theresa. Jackie made bedroom curtains out of old sheets, and we settled into our new home.

The only unpleasant thing about the apartment was the elderly lady who lived just beneath us. She didn't understand that people had to walk to get from one place to another and that such walking would create a noise emanating from her ceiling. She would demonstrate her displeasure by smacking her ceiling repeatedly with a broomstick or some such article. We tried to be as quiet as we could—even took to our bare feet—but she was somehow still able to determine that we were walking around and would immediately remind us by thumping vigorously. It began to get on my nerves after a couple of weeks, so I took my complaint to the good old resident manageress. She told me there was absolutely nothing anyone could do about that "old dear." She had driven three previous sets of tenants practically psycho, and we would just have to put up with it or move.

A couple of weeks later, we went away on vacation for a few days. When we returned around 9:30 in the evening and walked into the living room, the feverish banging commenced from below. I went calmly to my tool box, withdrew my large hammer, pulled back the living room rug, and proceeded to smash insanely on the floor. I was at it for a full five minutes before Jackie was able to wrest the hammer from my frantic hand. We listened. No response from below. I placed my ear to the floor. Perhaps I had given her a heart attack. No. She was down there cursing up a storm. There was no more banging with the broomstick thereafter. I had won the battle and made our apartment safe for democracy.

In May, I graduated with a double major in Economics and Foreign Affairs. After the ceremony, Jackie and I sat on a bench on the GWU campus, enjoying the balmy breezes of the late spring season. I was thoughtfully twisting my diploma when she said, "I'm almost six months now. What are your plans?"

"You know," I said, "twenty years ago, a high school diploma was a must. Ten years ago, a BA degree was essential. Today, I think one needs a graduate degree, especially when one is the father of almost two children." I patted her tummy tenderly, thinking what a fine boxer we would have, finally.

"I knew that would be your decision," she breathed.

"What do you think we should name our first boy?" I asked.

"How about Malcolm Jr.?"

"But that's not very original," I said. "What about Thurg?"

"What kind of a name is that? Was he a saint?"

"No, but it's better than a lot of names they're using in magazine articles these days," I replied.

I investigated the graduate program for that summer and learned that there were only two subjects I could take, and they were both in the evening. So I signed up for the courses and switched to full-time work at the Department of the Interior. The baby was born on August 29; it was a girl, of course. We decided to name her Catherine. By this time, Theresa was fifteen months old, still sucking her left thumb, and able to say sixty-seven words. When Jackie came home from the hospital, we added the second crib to our bedroom, preserving the rest of the apartment for gracious living.

In mid-September, I announced that my tipping and tilting days were over. "I hadn't noticed your drinking," Jackie said.

"It's not that," I replied. "When I notified Interior that I was returning to school full-time, my boss informed me that the part-time worker program in Geological Survey had been scratched."

"That is great," she said. "We have two children and you've lost your job. What are you going to do? Play ten nights a week in the band?"

"Not quite. It isn't that bad. I'll find another part-time job. One good thing: you're not pregnant."

"That reminds me. We have to increase the diaper order to thirty-six a day," she said.

Two weeks later, I started working in the afternoons as a library assistant in the Preparations Department of the District of Columbia Public Library. At about the same time, I switched from the hotel circuit to playing with a small combo at a roadhouse in Virginia. Jackie bought some materials for sequined ear-rings and brooches, at first with the idea of making inexpensive Christmas presents. They were most attractive, and when word got around, she started selling them among our friends and our friends' friends. By Christmas-time, she had quite a little business going, to the point where she was able to provide almost all of her own "pin" money. She liked to wear this homemade jewelry her-self and looked most sparkling when she accompanied me on the job that New Year's Eve.

It was quite a party that night. The roadhouse was named Hunters' Lodge. The job was scheduled from ten to two o'clock. The band was good and got better after it began receiving liberal offerings of beer from the guests. Jackie was sitting at a table located some thirty feet from the bandstand with a couple of orchestra wives. I peered through the smoked-filled hall and per-ceived that a handsome young man was standing by the table annoying her. *Of all the nerve,* I thought, but shrugged off my jealousy and continued my perfect percussive performance.

I tried to gauge my beer intake to coincide with the quitting hour. However, the owner announced at two o'clock that the music would continue until three. That handsome young man was apparently not annoying Jackie, but sitting next to her offer-ing a toast (to her health, no doubt). Somebody bought the band another round of beers, and we dug in our heels and struck out with, of all things, "The Two O'clock Jump." I always play drums better when I'm uninhibited. We played on and on—more beer. I looked for Jackie, but couldn't see her. Old Romeo had switched chairs so that his back was to me, blocking Jackie from my view. Soon it was five minutes to three. We played "Good Night, Sweetheart." The nightclub owner crawled onto the bandstand again and said, "As I get the message, you want more, so the joint stays open until four." Groans from the band, and another round of drinks; this time it wasn't beer. By then, I couldn't even see Jackie's table (because of the smoke).

For the next forty-five minutes, the hall was filled with the sweetest music this side of heaven. The air cleared momentarily, and I saw Jackie sending Lover Boy away from her table. I looked at my right hand and saw that it was holding a glassful of whiskey. The bandleader was grabbing for the microphone. It fell over on to the dance floor. Ray, the tenor saxophone man, picked it up and handed it to the leader, who announced, "Ladies and you other people—HA HA—it gives me great pleasure to announce the next number. It ain't for music lovers, but for all of you who like a lot of noise. I give you our drummer, Malcolm Lawrence, who will perform his best-ever rendition of 'Paradiddle Joe.'"

That idiot, I thought. I hadn't played that number since 1942, but I was game. Much to my surprise, the leader knew the words and sang the choruses. There followed a drum break beyond comparison. I pounded on everything in sight for fifteen minutes. One of my sticks sailed away and caught the piano man behind the ear. I grabbed another one and continued chopping away. I couldn't stop. Finally, someone pushed me off of my "drummer's throne," and I went backwards off the bandstand. I climbed back up and bowed to the applauding crowd. After our final version of "Good Night, Sweetheart," I whacked a terrific rim shot, thumped the bass drum as hard as I could, and smashed down on my biggest cymbal to signify the birth of a new year.

We packed up our instruments, wished everyone well, and started the drive back to Washington in the 1941 Chevy (on loan to us from Jackie's mother). The tenor saxophone man (Ray) was in the backseat with his wife. "What an evening," he said. "I'm glad you're driving." It had been snowing, but the roads weren't too bad. I crossed the Highway Bridge leading into town. At the end of the bridge where the road veers to the right, I discovered I had run into a slick patch. The car did a complete 360-degree spin and continued on in the direction of Washington. I was most surprised and relieved. From the backseat Ray said, "Man, you shouldn't clown around like that." We got up so late on New Year's Day we had to settle for "lunner," a late afternoon meal combining lunch and dinner, usually taking place five hours after brunch and conflicting most decidedly with high tea.

Late in April 1949, we invited a few friends in for a dinner party. The food and drink were delicious, and a good time was had by all. After the company left, Jackie washed the dishes. While I dried them, she went into the living room to relax. When I finished, I walked in and saw her asleep on the couch. She had loosened and removed some of her clothing. Her blouse was on a nearby chair and one of her silk stockings had landed on the picture rail some five feet above her head. "Really, Jacqueline," I said. "It's a good thing our friends have gone. Look at you. And how on earth did you manage to get your stocking up there?"

"I don't remember throwing it there," she said. "Maybe it was that wonderful wine."

I stood on the couch, grabbed the article, and brought it down. It was no silk stocking; it was a bat. We both jumped six feet in the air and started screaming. While I went searching for a broom, Jackie reached for her blouse and went to fetch the elevator operator, a young six-foot-three, 250-pound college student. He came bounding into the room, took one look at the bat, which was swooping frantically around the living-room, and said, "Leave that front door open."

"Don't you think it would be better to open a window instead?" I asked.

"Sure," he said, "but the door is for me."

With the three of us flailing away at the creature with brooms and mops, the bat finally flew out of the bedroom window. We thanked the elevator boy for his help, and when he left, we both fell onto the couch and into a fit of nervous laughter. "Things are not always what they seem," Jackie gasped.

"Yes. Imagine a silk stocking turning into a bat. You should have seen your face," I howled.

"My face? What about you—jumping up and down and raving like a banshee?"

"Well, at least the Lawrences were able to lick one more problem," I sighed.

"Yes, but we have another."

"Like what?"

"Like I'm pregnant again."

"Would you care for a cognac?" I inquired.

"I'd love one."

By mid-May, I had completed all of the requirements for a Masters degree in Government and Economic Policy except for my thesis. After three and a half years of studying, I decided to give myself a break for the summer and postponed working on that one final project. My objective was to locate a professional position with the government, and I began looking around for a job. At that time, however, the government was in the throes of an economy dive, and jobs were available only to those who had Civil Service status. The Civil Service registers for all professional positions in my field were either closed or suspended. I submitted applications with several agencies anyway and continued on at the library full-time.

On November 21, baby number three was born. It was another girl, and we named her Joan Marie. Catherine was fifteen months old and sucked the index finger of her left hand. She was a late talker, but quite a climber and spent a good deal of her time spinning around on the "Lazy Susan" in the middle of the dining room table. Theresa was two and a half then, had long curly blond hair, and managed to get into just about everything. Crib number three went into the bedroom, which began to take on the appearance of the nursery at Providence Hospital.

Postponing my thesis proved to be a big mistake. I had lost my momentum. Moreover, the inability to obtain a position in line with my education had dampened my incentive. Mid-1950 rolled around, and I still hadn't even picked a topic for my paper. At that point, the kids were really beginning to cause the walls of our apartment to bulge. Although our finances didn't warrant it, we went house hunting that summer and placed a deposit down for a three-bedroom colonial which was scheduled for completion in the fall.

The prospect of being a homeowner gave me a mental boost and led me to pursue a determined, albeit circuitous, method of acquiring a better job. The professional registers were still closed, but there was a demand for government clerk-typists. By working six months as a typist, one could obtain Civil Service status and become eligible thereafter for positions befitting one's qualifications. So, I borrowed a typewriter and a self-instruction book and pecked away at night. After three weeks, I worked up to forty words a minute. My concentration had been more on speed than accuracy, for in my first Civil Service typing test I made about forty errors. The next week when I took the test, my hands froze for a full thirty seconds and I didn't even try. The third time was better, but I didn't pass until the fourth. Having qualified as a genuine typist early in September, I submitted an application for a position as clerk-typist with my first-choice agency, the Department of State.

The prospect of having a new house had apparently also inspired Jackie. Early in October, when I told her I had been accepted by the Department of State, she announced that she was going to have another bouncing baby.

In the deal with State, I did not actually do any clerk/typing. I began as an economic editor for seven months and then vaulted into the professional ranks as an economic research analyst, writing in-depth studies on Western European countries. It was strange but true that just after I took the job with the State Department, offers started rolling in from Metropolitan Life, Proctor and Gamble, the National Intelligence Agency and Central Intelligence (CIA). But I stuck with State.

★ *Chapter Four* ★

SUBURBIA

We moved into the new house on December 23, 1950. I could think of 362 better dates on which a family should undertake such a project. However, we were all fired up with the spirit of Christmas and quickly forgot that the place had been promised for November 1. The house was situated some five miles from the District of Columbia border in Montgomery County, Maryland, in a tract of land known as "Oakview," a community development for some eight hundred homes. The name of the subdivision was derived from the fact that the area was loaded with oak trees. Actually, however, most of them were torn down during the construction period. Our house was located in a sort of valley, and we had the only flat piece of land in the immediate neighborhood.

At 8:00 A.M. on the morning of the 23rd, we packed ourselves and some odds and ends into the Chevy and started out for Oakview. When we reached the District line, someone said, "Where are the goldfish?" Back I went for the goldfish. The moving van was waiting for us when we finally arrived, and at nine o'clock the men started transferring our furniture (plus the snow that was falling on it) into 9802 Cahart Place, our new home.

After lunch, Jackie went off to do some Christmas shopping. While Theresa, Catherine, and Joan explored the new surroundings, I righted the furniture and undertook to scrub the kitchen and bathroom. At four o'clock, the electricity failed (that area of the subdivision was running on a generator at the time). I located a candle and went merrily on my working way. Jackie came home around six and said, "Who turned out all the lights? Are you trying to save money or something?"

"Not at all," I replied. "Come on up to the bathroom. The candle power is terrific."

The lights still hadn't come on by dinner time, and we had a nice meal by one candle light. While Jackie straightened up the dishes, I put the children to bed in the dark.

The next morning, I tried my hand at Christmas shopping. With my GI insurance dividend check, I bought a tree, an eighteen-pound turkey, some candles, and about thirty-five dollars worth of toys—most of which required assembling. In the evening, we had electricity again, and I had a job in the band (a horrible thought for Christmas Eve, but that's show business). Jackie's mother, aunt, and uncle-in-law came over and helped put all the things together. I came home at two in the morning, and they were still at it. I went out back, dragged in the Christmas tree and decorated it, while they filled the stockings with candy with care. Santa still did everything in those days.

The scene in the morning was one of merriment and mayhem as the little angels opened their presents. I had forgotten to buy Jackie one, but she never noticed in all the confusion. My father telephoned about ten and said he was on his way to take some pictures. We frantically straightened up the living room, turned on the tree lights, and waited. In he came, complete with the 8-mm movie camera and my mother.

By February, the snow had melted, and our neighbors began to stick their heads outside. Before moving in we had decided we wouldn't make friends with just anybody; we had to approve of them first. On our street there were twenty-two houses. As far as we could determine, the neighbors were just like us, except they had fewer children. There was a milkman, a Sears Roebuck accountant, an IBM wiring expert, a beer-truck driver, a labor union treasurer, a flautist with the National Symphony orchestra, a taxi driver, a garage mechanic, a professor at the University of Maryland, a lineman for the telephone company, a freelance writer, and a senior official (GS-15) with the Navy Department. *Our kind of folks,* I thought. And here I was, a GS-3 economic editor, starting out on my new career, with a new $12,000 house, three children and one on the way.

Confronted with this social situation (and a $10,500 mortgage), I decided to write my thesis. In mid-February, I went to the Federal Reserve Board of Governors and the U.S. Department of the Treasury and brought home all of their reports and other sources I could carry. I went out again, this time to a stationery store and bought one thousand five-by-seven inch cards, ten ball-point pens, and five thick writing tablets. I placed all this jazz on the antique desk (which we had put in the living room), went down to the basement, cleared a large area of working space, dragged out two ancient beds which needed refinishing, and went upstairs and poured myself a beer. I then set a deadline of May 1 to finish my thesis. It meant a forced holiday from my music work.

For the next ten weeks, I worked four nights a week on my paper and three nights scraping and varnishing the two beds. While this proved to be a wonderful system for alternating the mental and physical efforts, I found myself one evening calmly putting varnish on a five-by-seven card. Working until two or three o'clock each morning, I went from 185 to 154 pounds and managed to acquire twenty-seven warts on my left arm.

The title of my thesis was, "The Role of the Supported Government Securities Market in the Postwar Economy of the United States." It was an analysis of the monetary-fiscal problems confronting the government at the time. As I ground out each chapter, Jackie would type it. There were six, as I recall, and eleven grueling statistical tables. At 11:30 P.M. on May 3, we were sitting in the living room proofreading the last chapter when Jackie started squirming around on the couch. "What's the matter with you?" I asked.

"I'm having labor pains," she replied. "And they're ten minutes apart."

"Oh, for God's sake, we only have three more pages to go. Can't you wait? I'm already two days late getting this thing to the printer. Can you hold on?"

"O.K., but hurry," she said. "They could be eight minutes apart."

We finished the proofreading, and I raced her to Providence Hospital at midnight. You might know—the baby wasn't born until late the next morning. As soon as Jackie was awake, I went into her room and proudly told her that I had gotten my thesis to the printer on time and thanked her for all of her efforts. She rolled her eyes back into her head and said, "What do you think of your son?"

"What?" I yelped. "Nobody told me."

Good things come in threes. All in the same week, I had a son, I had finished my thesis, and I learned that my promotion to professional status had come through at the Department of State— and my wife wasn't even pregnant. I was then ready to face Oakview with pride.

While Thurg was a very tough and masculine name, we decided to call our first boy Malcolm. We gave him Edward as a middle name until a few weeks later when we happened to buy a family Bible on the installment plan and learned that Malcolm was a saint's name, so we dropped the Edward and made him Malcolm Jr. Joan was seventeen-and-a-half months old. Unlike the others, she didn't suck anything nor did she have any hair yet. Old Baldy, we used to call her. Catherine, at thirty-two months, was just about through the difficult two-year-old stage and continued to suck her finger when we weren't looking. Theresa was almost four years old, a big girl looking forward to school the following fall.

With the pressure lifted, my warts started failing off, and I went up to 175 pounds in six weeks. I resumed my part-time drumming career, switching back to the hotel circuit.

That summer, feeling most independent, I thanked my mother-in-law for the use of her 1941 Chevy and went into Silver Spring and bought a 1937 Chevy, a little something to haul our four kids around in. It was a nice car. Not yet fifteen years old, it had a broken speedometer, got stuck in second and reverse gears, and had a door on the driver's side that kept falling off. I used it, of course, to lug my drums around on my gay nights out with the orchestra.

One warm evening, right after work, I was booked for a 6:30 dinner-dance at the Washington Hotel. The temperature, as I recall, was around ninety-three degrees and the humidity likewise. Sweating up a storm, I pulled up in front of the hotel at 6:10, opened the car door on my side, and pulled the big bass drum out. The door fell flat into Fifteenth Street. I grabbed for it and dropped the drum. At that point, I glanced across the hood of the car and saw my State Department boss looking askance at me. The perspiration caused the coloring of my red bow tie to run down over my wilting white shirt and summer dress jacket.

The immaculate doorman yelled at me to get that heap out of the hotel doorway. I smiled at my boss and at the doorman, gracefully slid the car door under the car, unloaded the rest of my drums, carried them into the hotel lobby, came back out, reached under for the car door, replaced it onto the car, smiled at my boss (who was still standing there amazed) and at the doorman, and drove to the nearest parking lot. I ran back all the way (three blocks) threw the drums onto the elevator, got out at the top-floor restaurant, dragged the drums into the ballroom, unpacked them, and set them up by 6:26. The leader of the orchestra, whose name was Lee, said, "You were damned near late. Let's get here earlier next time." Just after that, the piano player came in looking calm, cool, and collected. He opened up his music and straightened his bow tie. Such a hard job he had. Leader Lee said, "A one and a two," and I never did tell the guys in the band (or the doorman) that my car got stuck in gear, and I had to have it hauled away from the parking lot wall at 2:00 A.M.

I mentioned earlier that our plot of land was flat and in sort of a valley. With this geographic situation, two things gravitated to our yard: water and children. About the water, I let it go for about six months, thinking it was the natural consequence of nature. When it began to look like a gorge, I made up my mind to close the gap. I took the kids and some cans in the car to a nearby gulch and picked up stones of all dimensions. We laid them in the gully and stopped our backyard from being the gutter of the neighborhood. Our little beavers made a few dams to protect my topsoil and grass seed, and we soon had the drainage problem licked.

About the children, they drifted down to our place and never went away—and I was glad. When we first arrived, there were about fifteen kids who could walk and talk. When we left—some seven years later—there were fifty-two of them, and they all called me "Pop." On our flat, now-filled-in lot we played baseball, football, tennis, volleyball, badminton, croquet, soccer, no bears out tonight, and a whole host of other games. I don't quite remember at which point my various children joined in the games, but they were messing around in there somewhere.

I was promoted in January 1952, and in February traded in the 1937 Chevy for a 1940 Olds, a car that had been driven backwards by two old ladies to church every other Sunday. It snowed that month, and everybody in the neighborhood contributed to the construction of a nine-foot snowman. Also, Jackie conceived our fifth child that month, but she didn't know it yet.

In April when she told me she was *avec enfant* (by this time she spoke broken French), I bought a dog just to have something different around the house. This was no ordinary dog; it was a cross between a boxer and a collie. It had the nose of a collie, the chest of a boxer, and the rear end of a collie. After seven months it weighed eighty-five pounds. Under the circumstances, we didn't know what to do with the ears and the tail, so we decided to leave them just the way they were. We called him "Stuffy." The collie in him made him a good dog around the children. The boxer in him made him a fine watchdog. He attacked me when I attacked the children and attacked the mailman when he tried to deliver letters up the street. Most of all, however, Stuffy thought he was a lap dog and used to sit on mine whenever I sat down. He ate fifteen pounds of beef and dog-meal each week, but we loved him. He was with us for six years.

Apparently Jackie thought one boy was enough for a while and on November 19 presented me with another girl. We were beginning to run out of girls' names that passed the dual test of being a saint's name and not already existing on either side of the family. We called her Louise and thereupon established the policy of one name only. The ages of the others were five and a half, four, three, and one and a half. One was finally in school. We stopped paying any attention at that point as to who sucked what, but we did notice that they were all beginning to eat more. It was not a rare occasion that I found myself hiding from the milkman and breadman toward the end of the month.

Our social life with the neighbors was a bit uneven, or perhaps I should say unfair from their point of view. Television was the big thing. When we visited their houses, the "idiot box" stayed on the whole time, and we all sat there and gaped at it for two or three hours. We didn't have a TV set, and when we entertained at our place everyone talked, of all things. To correct the situation, we finally bought a set in June 1953. The first program we watched, incidentally, was the coronation of Queen Elizabeth. Little did I know at the time that I would be shaking hands with her at Buckingham Palace five and a half years later.

By that summer, with five children, the Olds was getting a little crowded, so I traded it in on a '49 eight-passenger Ford station wagon. Everybody had a seat to himself, with one left over just in case. Between picnics, trips to the beach, and the weekly expeditions to the local shopping center, I spent all of my spare time putting coats of varnish on the wood-paneled sides of the wagon, but they still rotted away. It got so bad, I finally painted the whole thing with gray deck paint, and we ended up with the most distinctive-looking craft in the neighborhood.

For one reason or another, our tribe was healthy. Jackie attributed it to the excellent, balanced diet she furnished. I chalked it up to luck and to the fact that I wouldn't have been able to pay the bills if things had been otherwise. Whatever it was, we were glad and took great pride in the phenomenon that our children were apparently even immune to communicable childhood diseases.

No such immunity existed, however. Over an eight-week period in February and March 1954, there were fifteen cases of mumps, measles, and chicken pox at our house. The three diseases seemed to run around the place on conveyor belts, hitting first one child, then the other. The last one to fall ill had measles on her mumps and was the victim of much ribbing and laughter from the family. I had, incidentally, selected that period to paint the interior of the house, a difficult job in itself, but one made much more complicated by the task of constantly shifting beds with bodies in them. Fortunately, both Jackie and I had had all three diseases and were immune to them. Jackie had contracted something, however, and late in March—as I was peacefully cleaning and putting away all of my painting equipment—broke the news that child number six was on the way. I asked her to join me in a glass of turpentine.

I felt a little better about things on May 9, when I learned that I had been promoted again. I was happy with my job and convinced that I could make a successful career with the Department of State. With each promotion—and there had been three so far—I set my sights a little higher. The only trouble on the horizon was that the Department at the time was embarking on a reorganization to merge the classified professional personnel with the Foreign Service. Each employee electing to join the Foreign Service was, of course, making himself subject to overseas duty. Letters of invitation started going out that summer, and I was soon to receive mine.

In the meantime, on October 27, Jackie gave birth to another boy whom we named Joseph, after the saint of the same name. I was still sorry that there hadn't been a Saint Thurg. There we were, twenty-nine years old with six children. It was at that point that I received my letter from the Foreign Service Board of Examiners inviting me to join the team.

For several weeks, Jackie and I debated the pros and cons of life overseas. We were both thrilled with the prospect of serving abroad, but there were two important drawbacks. I felt that my income was insufficient to venture off to an unknown destination where living costs might be higher than in the United States.

Furthermore, three of the children were school-age, and there was uncertainty at the time concerning the level of government education allowances for dependents overseas. Consequently, I was reluctantly compelled to decline the offer on financial grounds.

On January 15, 1956, I was promoted again. By that time, legislation for overseas education allowances had been approved. I requested reconsideration for lateral entry into Foreign Service and was sworn in on July 21.

★ *Chapter Five* ★

PREPARING FOR OVERSEAS

Although an overseas assignment was not particularly imminent, we devoted our efforts beginning in the fall of 1956 to preparing for our future life abroad. I traded in our gray wooden craft for a 1954 all-metal Ford station wagon. We bought an elegant dining-room suite, five new beds, and some extra chests of drawers. We had the living room furniture reupholstered and became addicts of the auction houses. Our bids were successful on a silver tea service, a punch bowl set, some Staffordshire serving platters, and four steamer trunks.

The only missing item was a set of dishes. Early in 1957, a 120-piece set of French Limoges china came up on the block at an auction house in Georgetown. We both fell in love with the dishes at the showing. Jackie couldn't go with me on auction day, but gave explicit instructions that I was to come home with that china, even if I had to bid up to $2 per piece. The set went for $5 a piece. Equipped with some $250, I hung around to see what else there might be of interest. Guess what came up and what I took home? A 1956 RCA tape recorder and a set of left-handed golf clubs. Jackie had invited some of her friends to our place that afternoon and had told them of the great treasure I was about to bring in the door. In I walked with the tape recorder and golf clubs. You could have heard a pin drop.

In the midst of our period of preparation, I successfully sired another offspring, and Frances was born on September 7, 1957, our fifth girl.

We learned at the turn of the year that our overseas assignment would come up the following summer, so we sold our house and in February 1958 took a month-to-month lease in a small house in Falls Church, Virginia. Six of the kids slept dormitory-style in the attic, and baby Frances stayed with us in the only downstairs bedroom. We took turns eating in the breakfast nook and spent a great deal of our time tripping over furniture and packing cases. The house was up for sale during our stay there, and people kept wandering in to have a look. One day the doorbell rang, and Louise—who was five at the time—answered. Another couple to see the house. The dialogue went something like this:

> *"Hello, little girl. How are you?"*
> *"I'm five years old," said Louise.*
> *"Is your mother home?"*
> *"Sure."*
> *"May we see her?"*
> *"Sure."*
> *"May we come in?"*
> *"Sure," said Louise. And she led the couple down the hallway and said, "My mommy's in there."*

They opened the door and walked in, and the young man said, "We've come to see the . . ." Jackie looked up from the bathtub and set a new record for turning crimson.

We tried to keep ourselves as happy as we could in that little house. On the weekends, Malcolm and I usually got a great game of catch going. For a boy of seven, he was really very good at steaming the old ball across the front yard at me. I had to keep my eyes peeled to catch his fast ball a scant twenty-five feet from his delivery arm. For relief, we took to tossing the ball sky-high in assimilated pop-flies. One Sunday, when Malcolm and I had reached the pop-fly stage, Catherine, who was almost ten years old, pushed the front screen door open, leaped from the modest porch, and inquired ecstatically, "Can I catch one?"

"You mean, 'May I catch one?'" I replied.

"Yeah, that's what I mean. Throw the ball in the air," she said. I loaned her my mitt, limbered up my arm, and sent the ball high into the air. It soared up and up, blended in with the bright after-noon sun, and came down square in the middle of her forehead. She dropped the mitt and calmly walked into the house. On her way to the kitchen, her forehead altered from concave to convex. A few hours later, we determined that while she had a terrific headache, there was no concussion. Thank God! I knew then that Catherine would never play with the Yankees.

Then a sad day came. Our departure time was drawing near, so I placed an ad in the newspaper to sell my drums. For nineteen years I had been "thumping the tubs," but the time had finally come for me to hang up my sticks. After all, one couldn't be a diplomat and go around beating drums in strange countries, or at least in some strange countries. Among those who answered the ad was a wide-eyed boy of fourteen, who became even more wide-eyed when he saw my drums—mother-of-pearl finish, assorted Turkish cymbals—all for $250. The boy's parents said all they had was $225. "Sorry," I said, "but the price is $250."

"I'll pay you the rest from my first jobs," he announced from behind the drums.

"Never mind, son," I said. "They're yours for $225. With a spirit like that, you shall one day be as great a boxer—uh, I mean drummer—as I was." Out went the drums and a part of my life. Jackie didn't drop any tears, however. Because of my music career, she hadn't had a decent night out on a weekend since she was sixteen years old. "It's the end of an era," I said. "I suppose I'll never play drums again."

"That's too bad, Malc," she replied, wondering how much the tape recorder and golf clubs would bring in.

In March we got the word that London, England, was to be our post. "Oh, Malc, isn't that wonderful?" said Jackie.

"But I've already been there," I said.

"Yes, I know, now I can see that quaint little village near your wartime rest home." I made a mental note to forget just where that little place was.

Realizing that this would be our last opportunity to enjoy the celebration of the independence of the United States of America in the United States of America for some years to come, I ventured out and purchased thirty dollars worth of fireworks. Two families down the street did the same thing, and we all agreed to meet in front of our house at eight o'clock to shoot off our collective efforts. We had a community cook-out beforehand, and six grown-ups washed down hamburgers with Tom Collins, while the thirteen children did the same with two and a half cases of assorted soft drinks.

At the appointed hour, we started setting off fireworks like fury. What with firecrackers, flares, snakes, rockets, and Roman candles, it looked and sounded like the American Revolution all over again. We had only been at it for fifteen minutes when our next-door neighbors up the street, an elderly couple obviously conservative in taste, approached the scene and asked us to please be quiet. We explained the significance of the Fourth of July to them, but they were unimpressed. A heated discussion followed, during which the elderly couple was put on notice that if they didn't go peacefully back to their premises, they would be recommended for investigation by the Un-American Activities Committee. At length, they returned to their front porch, sat down in rocking chairs, folded their arms, and glared at our little band of patriots as we relit the punk and resumed our demonstration of good citizenship.

Everything went fine until Joan, under the misapprehension that she was holding a spray fountain, lit a Roman candle which was pointed in the direction of the elderly couple's porch. A succession of beautifully-colored fireballs brightened up their solitude. The old man went into the house and calmly called the police. By the time the uniformed officers of the law reached our front yard, Joseph, Louise, and four other dear little offspring of our friendly group were innocently holding sparklers, and the six peace-loving grown-ups were huddled near the house quietly singing patriotic songs. The policemen took a look at our group and departed. It's hard to believe, but the old couple didn't even wave good-bye when we departed for England later that month. There's no accounting for tastes.

The movers came on July 27 and placed most of what we owned in a steel lift-van. The rest of the things, which Jackie had determined we "needed on voyage," were packed in fourteen wooden crates, four steamer trunks, and ten large suitcases. These were picked up that afternoon and taken to Pier 86 in New York. We took four suitcases (containing night garments and toothbrushes) and moved in with Jackie's mother for four nights. I won't attempt to describe our stay there because Jackie had packed my pajamas in the lift-van. At 10:00 P.M. on July 31, we waved good-bye to one and all (we thought) and boarded the night-sleeper at Union Station in Washington, headed for New York and the SS *America*.

I don't know about the other people on the car, but we certainly didn't get much sleep. None of the children had ever been on a train before and matters were made worse, I suppose, by the exciting prospect of boarding a ship the next day. The kids roamed in and out of the four sleeping compartments and complained about one thing or another. Most of the night they were all in Mommy's and Daddy's "room," which at best accommodated two people. By four in the morning, Jackie and I had finally settled them down, gotten undressed, and we placed our weary heads on the pillows. Just before 5:00 A.M., Jackie shook me and said, "Malc . . . Malc, wake up. We're in Philadelphia."

"So what? We're going to New York."

"I know, but I was born here," she said.

"In the station?" We couldn't go back to sleep after that. I lifted Frances off my stomach, got dressed, and watched the sun rise as the train plied the rails to New York.

That afternoon at Pier 86, we were surprised by a little committee consisting of my mother, sister, and brother and his family; Jackie's mother, sister, and brother; a friend-of-the-family priest from Philadelphia; and a family of neighbors from Falls Church. All of those jokers had surreptitiously driven to New York during the morning to wish us *bon voyage.* At 2:00 P.M., the whole gang boarded the ship and helped us find our three staterooms on Upper Deck. I ordered Cokes for the children and drew out a quart of bourbon (from one of the night garment cases) for the grown-ups. By and by, the all-ashore horn sounded, the band played "Anchors Aweigh," and amidst a flurry of handshakes, kisses, and tears, our families and friends made their way down the gangplank to line up and wave us off. Looking down and throwing streamers from an open deck were Theresa, age eleven; Catherine, ten; Joan, nine; Malcolm, seven; Louise, five; and Joseph, just under four. Frances, at eleven months, was in her mother's arms. Jackie waved to her mother, I waved to mine, and then I visualized a face that wasn't there—the face of my father, who had passed away on April 10, 1957. The ship's horn sounded, and the SS *America* eased slowly away from the pier, ocean bound.

One nice thing about a large family is that nobody ever gets lonely. Moreover, there is usually so much confusion that wherever the family is, it seems like home. At least Jackie thinks so, and no matter where we are or for how long, she always opens up everything available and sets up housekeeping. We were to be on the ship for only seven days, but by the first night, she had distributed the contents of the four steamer trunks, all of the suitcases, and most of the wooden crates throughout our three little staterooms. Part of her reasoning was that it was expensive to have laundry done on the ship, and the children needed two outfits for every day—one for play and one for dress-up. I quickly multiplied two outfits by seven kids by seven days and came up with a total of ninety-eight outfits. With all that mess, it took me quite a while to find a pair of clean socks.

Anyway, those of us who walked managed to get dressed up the first evening. We put an eight-ounce bottle of milk in Fran's mouth and paraded into the dining room. Not having had much to eat since the night before, we partook in just about everything on the menu. After dinner, we checked on Frances, found her okay, and took the other children on an hour and a half walk all over the ship to wear out their little legs and hopefully induce sleep. It worked. We put them to bed and around ten o'clock went up to the ballroom. I spotted three fellows I knew in the Meyer Davis Orchestra and sat in on drums for about an hour, while Jackie danced with a sixty-five-year-old millionaire horse dealer. When I joined her at the table, she said, "Some end of an era." For the remainder of the nights on the cruise, we continued the deck-walking bit with the children and ended up in the ballroom, but out of deference to Jackie (who, after all, couldn't talk about horses every night), I laid off the drums.

The trip was a most relaxing vacation for us. The weather was perfect and the food delicious. The children spent most of their time in the swimming pool and at the movies. When bored with those pastimes, they rode up and down the ship's elevators. That activity brought a big smile and a large upturned hand from the elevator boy at the end of the voyage.

On the morning of August 8, we docked at Southampton.

Here I am at age three.

A 1936 photo of our family at our home, 114 Longfellow Street N.W., Washington, D.C. My dad, Lester A. Lawrence, Sr., is seated. Top from left to right is me, my sister Patricia, my mom Hetty, and my brother Lester, Jr.

At age 13, strolling on F Street N.W., in downtown Washington, 1938.

Here I am at age 15 launching my music career as a left-handed drummer playing right-handed, spring of 1941.

On drums with the Wally Hughes 13-piece band, fall of 1942, at the Washington Hotel, Washington, D.C.

Jackie and I at our senior prom, Coolidge High School, February, 1943.

Here we are celebrating our first anniversary of dating at the Hotel Roosevelt Victory Room, listening and dancing to the music of Teddy Powell's band, June 12, 1943.

Air Force basic training in Miami Beach, December, 1943.

Crew 35, 94th Bomb Group, 8th Air Force, Bury St. Edmunds, England, January, 1945. Top row, left to right: Bill Edmisson, Tail Gunner; Malcolm Lawrence, Radio Operator-Gunner; Randall Bennett, Waist Gunner; James Elliott, Engineer; Howard Wallace, Toggleer. Bottom row, left to right: Max Gianelloni, Ball Turret Gunner; James Benson, Co-Pilot; James Shipman, Navigator; Noel Cheatam, Pilot. A great team!

Jackie liked my first car, a 12-cylinder Lincoln Zephyr, March, 1946.

But she liked her engagement ring better, June, 1946.

Our wedding at St. Matthew's Cathedral, Washington, D.C.,
November 27, 1946.

Jackie and I with our first three: Theresa, Catherine and Joan, May, 1950.

Our first house, 9802 Cahart Place, Oakview, Maryland, 1951-1957, where scads of neighbor kids gathered for fun and games. Jackie's mother, Elizabeth Drullard, joins us in a backyard party.

Theresa, Catherine and Joan help make our famous snowman in
February, 1952.

With my mother, sister Pat and brother Lester in 1952.

Malcolm Jr. having a ball at Bay Ridge, Maryland, 1954.

The kids enjoying our first Ford station wagon, Easter, 1955.

Being sworn into the U.S. Foreign Service, July 21, 1956.
I am third from the right. Witnessing the ceremony to the right of the
group is Ambassador Raymond Hare.

With our wonderful family dog, Stuffy, half boxer and half collie, 1957.

My last paid job playing the drums, March, 1958.
Lee Maxfield orchestra, leader is Bill Moon on saxophone.

First night on the SS *America* just after I sat in on drums with the
Meyer Davis orchestra, July, 1958.

Enjoying the Captain's Dinner as we approach England on the
SS *America*, July, 1958. Left to right: me, Jackie, Theresa, Louise,
Catherine, Joan, Malcolm Jr. and Joseph. Baby Frances was taking a nap.

Settling in at Eden Lodge on Wescott Road, our home in
Dorking, England, August, 1958.

Chapter Six

OUR ENGLISH COUNTRY HOME

Before arriving in London, we had to learn the differences between the British Isles, the United Kingdom, Great Britain, and England. Many people think these terms are interchangeable, but they're not. I provide below a simple tabulation, which all readers are invited to clip and carry around in their wallets and pocketbooks:

England is England. England plus Wales plus Scotland equals Great Britain. Great Britain plus Northern Ireland equals the United Kingdom. The United Kingdom plus the Irish Republic equals the British Isles.

The Irish Republic was officially proclaimed independent in 1949. Thus, the area to which I was accredited is the United Kingdom, frequently referred to as the UK. The United Kingdom is one-thirty-eighth the size of the United States, but has a population one-fifth as large as ours. This yields a population density eight times that of the United States, which tends to make things a little crowded in the UK, especially at Piccadilly Circus during rush hours. The American Embassy is at Grosvenor (pronounced Grov-nah) Square, about one mile from Piccadilly Circus, in the heart of London's West End. So much for geography and demography.

We traveled to London by boat-train and arrived at Waterloo Station in the late afternoon. We were met by my boss, who had brought his car, an Embassy station wagon, and a two-ton truck to transport us to the St. James's Court Hotel, a delightful old place two blocks from Buckingham Palace. We were given a wing in the ground floor rear court, containing five bedrooms and two baths. Jackie unpacked everything by dinner time (of course), and we proceeded to the hotel dining room for our first meal in Britain (that's short for Great Britain). After eating, I looked at the bill, pro-rated my costs per week and decided that we had better look for a house right away.

Fortunately, an Embassy Officer telephoned that very night and told me he had the perfect house for us. He had lived in it for four years and was moving out that weekend. When he arrived in England in 1954, he had looked at more than fifty houses, and this was the best deal he had been able to locate. It had a lounge (living room), a dining room, a sitting room, a sun room, a kitchen, a scullery (a room for washing dishes), a larder (pantry), six bedrooms, two bathrooms, and a two-car garage. It also had a beautiful front semi-circular driveway and a huge L-shaped garden (yard) in the rear. What's more, the rent was reasonable.

"Sounds great," I said. "Where is it?"

"Only twenty-seven miles from London, in Dorking, Surrey," he replied.

What with fast trains and my even faster, sleek station wagon, distance was no problem. "When can I see it?" I inquired.

"Well," he said, "I've already told the landlady that you're going down tomorrow, but there's one problem: she doesn't like children. Last year, my son broke a favorite plant in her garden, and she's never forgiven us. How many kids do you have?"

"Seven," I replied.

"Any sweet little girls?"

"I have five. What's on your mind?"

"Well, take two of your nicest and tell her all the rest are just like them."

The next day, Jackie dressed Joan and Louise (our two youngest walking females) in their Sunday best. By that time, I had returned with a left-hand-drive car. The two angels and I waved good-bye to the rest of the family, and I drove to Dorking on the left-hand side of the road. It was easy for me, of course, because I was left-handed. In a left-hand-drive car, the foot pedals are the same as in an American car, but the gear shift and turn indicator lever are just the reverse. The open road driving was a snap, but pulling off from intersections I had a hell of a time getting the turn indicator into second gear.

We made it to the house somehow. It was situated on the west outskirts of Dorking, on the Westcott Road leading to Guildford. A veritable English country house, it stood well back from the road on beautiful formal grounds. As we got out of the car, I reminded Joan and Louise not to pick flowers or pull up any shrubs. We met the landlady, who was a delightful old gal pushing eighty. I decided then and there, subject to Jackie's approval, that the house was just what we wanted. While the landlady and I were sitting in the lounge negotiating the deal over a glass of Scotch, I noticed that my colleague from the Embassy was stomping all over the house with two men. I asked the landlady what was going on, and she explained that he was witnessing the "marching-out inventory." It sounded very official and expensive to me. I filled her glass and excused myself for a moment.

I had an aside with my friend and asked about the inventory. He explained that the house was partly furnished, which meant that the furniture was falling apart. When we finished laughing, he went on to tell me that in England there is a "marching-in inventory" of the furnishings in a rented house. The owner hires an agent, the prospective tenant hires an agent, and everybody goes through the house noting the condition of the furniture and fittings. The list of the owner's agent describes everything as being in almost perfect condition, while that of the tenant's agent depicts everything as scratched, broken, or dilapidated. They are then compared and consolidated, and entries emerge, such as, "Buffet in dining room, old (circa 1890), fair condition with perfectly beautiful scratches making it of near antique value." This would be the compromise between "priceless family heirloom" and "junk," he explained. He also told me he hadn't used a stick of the landlady's furniture in four years, but had stored it all in the loft (attic) the day after he moved in. He had just brought it down two days ago and was most interested to find out what the consolidated list of the "marching-out inventory" would look like and how much money he was going to have to pay just because the stuff was four years older. I thanked him and went back into the lounge, where the landlady was pouring herself a third Scotch.

"Have another?" she said.

"Don't mind if I do," I replied. "I have a question for you."

"What is it, sonny?" she asked.

"I just happened to pass the former tenant in the hall and he said there was both a marching-in and a marching-out inventory. Would it be possible for me to use his marching-out as my marching-in?"

"It isn't the same thing, you know. It would be most irregular," she replied. "'I've been renting this house since my husband died, and I've always had a marching-in and a marching-out for each occupier."

"What about a marching-out-in-inventory?" I asked.

"It's a deal," she said, filling both our glasses.

"That's better than a marching-in-out-outventory. But I'm most concerned about the garden. Last year, one of the tenant's children let a ball roll right into one of my favorite plants. We had quite a row about it."

"Goodness gracious!" I said. "How terrible!"

"Indeed! Are you certain the rest of your kiddies are as nice as these two?" she asked, glancing over at Joan and Louise, who were sitting beneath their temporary halos.

"But of course," I replied.

We moved into our new mansion on Saturday, August 16, 1958. Four weeks later, after our station wagon and household effects had arrived, I put all of the landlady's priceless furniture in the loft. We enrolled six of our seven children in St. Joseph's Priory, a local Catholic convent school, and purchased six little brown uniforms to go with it. (I haven't mentioned it yet, but everybody in our family is Catholic, except me. Thus, Jackie and I had a mixed marriage, to which I agreed because the priest had promised, "God will provide.") We spent the better part of our evenings that first winter helping the children with their homework. It was difficult enough doing math in pounds, shillings, and pence, but much worse when our older "babies" would line up for help in algebra, chemistry, physics, Latin, and English literature. Jackie and I would somehow split the homework chores, and at ten o'clock I would call it quits because I had much more important work to do: bank the fire.

If we had arrived in England in mid-December, we probably would have looked at more than one house. I doubt if this place had ever experienced any real heat in wintertime. It had what is known as a boiler in the kitchen, leading to nine small radiators, all on inside walls to save on piping, I suppose, plus the logic that there is little sense in putting radiators near cold windows. Elsewhere in the house, there were two open fireplaces, five formerly open fireplaces with gas-heat installations, and two formerly open fireplaces with electrical units. Banking the fire was but the last of the things I had to do during a typical winter day to make that place habitable.

First of all, I got up at six o'clock, which was bad enough. I went out back to the coal-house and carried in five shuttlefuls of "ovals" for the kitchen boiler. Having renewed the fire there and emptied the ashes, I went around the house lighting the gas fires and turning on the electric fireplaces. Then I plugged in four thirteen-amp electric space heaters at strategic spots around the house and crawled back into bed. At 6:45, when the alarm went off, Jackie would awaken and say, "God, but it's cold in here."

"Never mind, dear. Just get up and fix some nice breakfast," I suggested. She arose from bed in her sexy long woolen underwear, slipped something appropriate over it and went downstairs to put on the coffee. In the meantime, I dashed through the cold hallway to the colder bathroom. The water came from a geyser, a gas hot water heater which was located a full four feet above the tub. The water was hot enough at the source, but by the time it hit the freezing tub, the heat was completely neutralized. Anyway, after I shaved and bathed, I got dressed and dragged the kids downstairs for the scrumptious breakfast Jackie had prepared. At 7:25, I jumped up from the table to catch the bus to meet my train. The children were able to linger over their porridge for another fifteen minutes before venturing across a cow pasture to school. When everyone had left, Jackie took Frances into the kitchen, poured another shuttleful of ovals into the boiler, put her feet on it, and sat there with her second cup of coffee. On weekends, things were much better. I put "Number One" house coal in the two open fireplaces, which in addition to all the other sources of heat, managed to bring the temperature of our place clear up to sixty-five degrees Fahrenheit.

Situated southwest of the London Green Belt and nestled in a valley between Box Hill, Leith Hill, and Ranmore, Dorking is a town of some twenty-two thousand people. It has very little industry of its own, aside from the normal services, and is known as a "dormitory town" because a fairly large percentage of its working population is employed in London. While some of the breadwinners drive "up to London" each day, the most popular means of transport seems to be by the commuter train.

I became a rail commuter myself, and it took me quite a while to get used to the austere atmosphere. As far as I know, there are no regulations spelling out the conduct expected of one on a British commuter train. I began taking the 7:46 A.M. train from the Dorking North Station and quickly learned the pattern of etiquette. At 7:40, the platform was lined with hundreds of businessmen, all with morning newspapers folded under their arms. Each person had his special, seemingly reserved spot on the platform. Words of greeting were exchanged, such as "Morning" and "Luv'ly day" (even when it was raining). Some groups of men were having substantive conversations about business and world affairs. When the train pulled in, each man, positioned by his customary carriage door (there is a door for each section of seats), entered the train and sat in his customary seat. There were still some grunts and nods of greeting so long as the train remained stationary, but once it pulled off, up went the newspapers, and not a word was heard until the train rolled into Waterloo Station forty-three minutes later. The procedure was exactly the same on the 6:26 P.M. return train, except everyone read evening papers.

In my more than two years of travel on commuter trains, only one person spoke to me, and he was an Italian. As I was sitting in my customary seat one evening, I heard a voice booming from across the aisle, "You're an American, aren't you?" I looked sheepishly around my paper and detected that other papers were being lowered.

"Yes," I answered quietly, hoping that reply would satisfy him once and for all.

"I thought so. I could tell by the clothes." By this time, I really felt conspicuous.

"What kind of work you do?" he hollered. This is the sort of question one would not ask in England until one has been acquainted with a person for at least six months and one would certainly never ask it on a train.

"I work with the American Embassy," I said as softly as I could.

"Oh, you're one of them diplomats." Everyone felt sorry for me, and I'm sure they all wanted to have this man put off the train at the next stop. Their reading had been interrupted, and my private life had been exposed. My reply to his last statement was so soft, my Italian friend couldn't hear it, so he lost interest and fell asleep. My fellow travelers settled back down to their newspapers, and I had the feeling they could hardly wait to get home to tell their wives about that most unusual incident on the train.

I should quickly point out that British commuters are not completely inhuman and unemotional. Whenever a lovely young girl entered the car and positioned herself on the seat in the fashion that lovely young girls do that sort of thing, not one of the commuters would miss taking in the view. However, each one took turns looking, and not one would dare be caught by the others as he feasted his eyes on the female. They had an uncanny way of knowing exactly where everybody else's eyeballs were. I, of course, learned to know where all the eyeballs were too and outsmarted them at their own game.

The most comical incident I witnessed on a commuter train was when a drunk carrying a large stack of newspapers got on the 6:26 at Waterloo. He sat in the center of a three-seater and put on quite a show. He placed the pile of papers on his knees and proceeded to read them one at a time. Unlike the trained and sober commuter, he was unable to unfold and refold his papers neatly and quietly. As he finished looking at each one, he balled it up and jammed it inside the front of his overcoat, talking loudly to himself all the while. The combination of his activity and the serenity elsewhere on the car led me to break out with a smile. Everybody stared at me. As the man stood up to get off the train at Leatherhead, the entire supply of newspapers fell out from under his overcoat onto the floor. Leaving the papers lying in the middle of the compartment, he staggered off the train. The train pulled off, and there was dead silence.

In November, Jackie and I, along with other Embassy officials and their wives, attended an evening reception at Buckingham Palace. I left work early so I could pick Jackie up and drive back to London. I collapsed the middle seat of our wagon so she could sit and spread out her long green taffeta dress. Folks on the top of the double-decker buses must have wondered what was happening and where we were going. At the Embassy we switched to a limousine and passed through the palace gates. We entered the great foyer and ascended one of the twin staircases to the entertainment area.

Upstairs, everyone lined up on two sides of a long hallway waiting to be greeted by Queen Elizabeth and the other members of the royal family. I stood just behind a more senior Embassy officer. Prince Philip moved along our side, stopping to chat with the guests. When he reached our spot, he asked the officer in front of me what his name was. He was stunned and could not say his name. I whispered it into his ear, and he repeated it to Philip. After the reception line broke up, we moved to the ballroom and enjoyed drinks, finger food, and music. What a night! During our drive back to Dorking, Jackie and I recalled the fun time we had and fantasized about inviting the Queen and Philip down to our place.

Each Saturday, I took the walking children into town for a shopping tour. We took a dozen string bags to at least a dozen stores; there were no supermarkets. On our first trip to the meat shop, I asked for roast beef. The butcher brought forward a twelve-pound rolled roast and asked where he should cut it. I said, "Nowhere. I'll take the whole thing." He was shocked and asked, "What about my other customers?" He placed orders for more beef for subsequent Saturdays. After the meat shop, we traipsed to the other stores for fruits and vegetables, canned goods, milk, bread, and whatever hardware we needed. We then stopped at Woolworth's for those of us with a sweet tooth. When our string bags were full, we dumped everything in the station wagon and wended our way home.

On March 9, 1959, I was promoted and eagerly awaited the increase in salary. However, Jackie was clever in devising new ways to spend money. She told me she was going to have a little English baby.

"Jacq, I realize, what with commuting three hours a day and being at the office five days a week, I haven't been seeing much of you lately. But an English baby? Really!"

"Don't be silly, Malc. It's yours, of course," she said.

"But how can you get pregnant in a foreign country?"

"You didn't spend all night banking the fire, you know," she remarked coyly. I smiled inwardly, realizing that if I hadn't banked the fire, I wouldn't have been able to tell Jackie from an iceberg and that perhaps from the point of view of our marriage, it was better that I had banked the fire and been able to tell Jackie from . . . oh well, you know what I mean.

While child number eight was on the way, I built a hi-fi record cabinet. I had brought all sorts of equipment overseas with me—a radio chassis, a record player, a 1956 RCA tape recorder, and six speakers. That spring, I went into town and bought some one-by-tens and two-by-twos, lots of one-half inch plywood panels, some hinges, wood stain, and a whole bunch of nails. My design called for a piece large enough to hold all of the equipment plus two hundred LPs and a good supply of 45 rpm records and tapes. The measurements were five feet wide, three and a half feet deep, and three and a half feet high. I built the thing in the garage and completed it in seven weekends. There had been one small oversight on my part, however, which I didn't notice until the day five of us tried to cart the box into the house. It wouldn't fit through the front door. I removed the door, but it still wouldn't clear by an inch. I almost chopped the damn thing into pieces then and there. But I calmed down and patiently disassembled portions of it and put it together again in the living room. It looked considerably larger there than it had in the garage. After much argument, Jackie let it stay, but gave it the affectionate nickname of "Malcolm's coffin."

That summer, it seemed as though a couple of other members of the family were trying to beat me to the coffin. Catherine, still caught up in her desire to climb at age ten, tried to make it from her upstairs bedroom window to the ground. She slipped off a ledge, fell onto the greenhouse roof, broke two large panes of glass, bounced off, and landed on her back in a flower bed, breaking, I might add, not one but two plants. Joseph wandered into the house and asked, "Mommy, why is Cathy sleeping in the side garden?" The fall had knocked her unconscious, but she came around in a few minutes and reported no broken bones. The explanation of her adventure was that she was trying to save herself "in case of fire." About a week later, Joan fell out of a tree and broke her arm, but no plants. Needless to say, these two incidents were followed by long mealtime lectures on safety precautions.

The summer of 1959 redeemed most of our ills and chills. It was the longest and hottest summer on record for England, so the local inhabitants said. Cars overheated, cows died, people went bathing every day, tar melted on the roads, the grass burned out, and—best of all—our house temperature went above seventy degrees all by itself. Despite the heat, our garden was maintained in glorious, flaming technicolor through the persistent efforts of the landlady's gardener, who had worked on the place for more than thirty years. In the formal part of the L-shaped grounds, just to the rear of the house, were two diamond-shaped flower beds containing all varieties of irises, bordered by deep purple phlox. Running the length of the garden on either side of the flower beds were long arbors of the finest English roses, carefully cultivated to produce magnificent blooms. The garden was spread wider by two gravel paths, bordered by tree roses, lilacs, and fruit trees. Skirting all that were twelve-foot hedges. At the bottom of the formal garden was a low full hedge of lavender, anchored at the ends by two 150-foot poplar trees, the landmarks of our property. Beyond this, completing the "L," was a 60-by-120-foot roughhouse field on which the Lawrence family held fun and games and attempted to do each other in all summer long.

The good weather was still going strong on September 19 when Jackie interrupted a hot game of soccer with the announcement clear across the formal garden that she was having pains ten minutes apart. With the hospital some forty miles away, we jumped into the car and raced for the U.S. Air Force Base at South Ruislip, Middlesex, ostensibly to have a baby. As it turned out, we could have walked backwards on our knees and still have had plenty of time. Ann, our little daughter number six, wasn't born until twenty-one days later.

For those who are extremely interested in this sort of thing, Jackie's water broke on September 19, and the baby became lodged in the birth canal. The baby's shoulders were too large to permit the use of forceps, and the body was too low to chance a Caesarean section. The doctor told us we would just have to wait until the forces of nature came into play. And wait we did. While Jackie faced the prospect of becoming ten months pregnant, I made a ninety-mile trip every day by car, from Dorking to London in the morning, from London to Ruislip in the late afternoon, and from Ruislip to Dorking in the evening. When I arrived home at night, the kids would ask me if it was a boy or a girl. "It's a nothing yet," I would reply. Finally, on October 10, Ann arrived. She weighed ten and half pounds, clearly our largest to date. I told Jackie that if our next baby was any bigger than that, she would have to get someone else to have it. "Who did you have in mind?" she inquired.

If the summer of 1959 had been a particularly hot one, the fall of that year was probably one of the foggiest. Late in November, after Jackie had recovered from arduous Ann, I took her up to the big city to celebrate. We had dinner, went to a play, and topped off the evening at the Talk o' the Town. We spilled out of the club at 1:30 in the morning and didn't know where we were. It wasn't the drinks; it was foggy, so foggy we could barely see across Shaftesbury Avenue. We finally managed to locate the car and set off for Dorking.

The yellow-cast lights served as fairly adequate visual aids out of London, but after that, things really got bad. The cars were creeping along at five to ten miles an hour. The fog lifted a little beyond Putney, and I could make things out some forty to fifty feet ahead of our car. Jackie remarked that she could see the heads of several drivers sticking out on the right-hand side (of the car, that is). A Jaguar zoomed by at about forty miles an hour.

"Some kind of an idiot," I remarked and continued creeping behind the leaders.

When we approached Leatherhead (about four-fifths of the way home), I realized I was still following the same bunch of cars. We made our way around the town bypass, and I became very brave. "I'm going to pass," I told Jackie. Pulling out to the right, I overtook six cars and became the leader. At that crucial point, the fog turned as thick as pea soup, and I was leading my little group downhill into a valley. In front, nothing but darkness. I slackened my speed and planted my eyes against the windshield. Jackie commented, "I don't think you should have passed, Malc." I felt slightly better when my eyes became accustomed to the dark and increased my pace to ten miles an hour. Everybody behind me seemed to be happy too. At a tricky turn, I smartly maneuvered the car to the left. About five minutes later, everyone started honking his horn. I soon learned why when I approached an absolute dead-end at a farmer's house. You can imagine the commotion and cursing as the seven cars backed out of the country lane. The good farmer helped us with his lantern and commented that it wasn't the first time a bunch of drunks had turned into his place in the fog.

In England, a high price is placed on privacy, and we were no exception with our twelve-foot hedges on either side of the house. Perhaps this was the reason no one in the neighborhood took notice of us until we had lived there a full sixteen months. Then, one day in mid-December 1959, a neighbor saw me in town and said, "I say, aren't you the new people who just moved in?"

"I'm one of them," I replied.

"Well my wife was saying just the other day we ought to get together with our new neighbors. Do you have children?"

"We have eight. Haven't you heard them yet?"

"Well . . . yes," he said. "We're having a few friends down from London on December 19. How about dropping in for a drink?"

"We'd be delighted," I said. "What did you say your name was?"

"Craven-Roper."

"Glad to know you, Cray. My name Is Malcolm Lawrence."

I told Jackie I had met a man named Cray von Roper who had invited us to a Christmas drink. "What a funny name for an Englishman," she said. We went to Cray's house for the drink and thought it very strange that everyone called him Richard.

A few weeks later, we held a dinner party in honor of Richard and his wife. Richard was a solicitor, and we carefully selected the other guests to assure a good mixture. We had an insurance firm partner, a director of an automobile dealership, and the owner of a retail clothing store—and, of course, their wives. That night, Jackie and I witnessed the social class system in action. Everybody talked to us, but the guests did not talk to each other. The men obviously had only two things in common: they worked in London and lived in Dorking. Moreover, they had been to different schools and had dissimilar accents, a great social divider in England. However, the roast beef, jacket potatoes, asparagus, and wine did go well together, and by the time dessert and the liqueurs rolled around, we got on the subject of World War II, and everybody began talking excitedly about that to himself, especially Cray—I mean Richard—who out-shouted all of us in telling his exploits as an air-raid warden.

We struck up a great friendship after that party with the insurance firm partner, David Jago, and his wife. We had much in common, or perhaps I should say many. We had eight children, and they had seven. That fact alone was enough to draw us together, but they were truly enjoyable people, and we had great fun for many months comparing notes and participating in joint outings. David had every imaginable thing in his garden for his children, and mine, to enjoy. He had a network of ropes rigged in trees, swinging tires, an archery set, and a horse. However, the project that inspired our children most was David's family Christmas play in December 1959. After the Lawrence children had witnessed that performance—written, produced, and directed by the parents and enacted by David's children—they insisted that we stage our own family play, and it couldn't wait until next Christmas either.

For several days, there was much discussion at our house about a story to serve as a basis for such a play. Theresa, Catherine, and Joan all tried their hands at writing an original. They finally decided that I should rewrite "Jack and the Beanstalk" and make it really funny. This was basically an almost impossible task for me, because I thought the story was pretty funny as originally written. Nevertheless, I tried my first comedy play. My approach was to Americanize the story and include such expressions as, "Fee, Fie, Foe, Fud! I smell an American's blood." It was loaded with all sorts of humorous passages like that, and everybody laughed their heads off when I read the whole thing.

The next step was to set the stage and arrange for the first rehearsal, including chairs for the future audience. After that, the trouble began. Everybody wanted to be Jack, probably because Jack had the biggest part. It was finally resolved that Theresa should be Jack, because she was the oldest. Catherine was Jack's mother. Malcolm was the giant. Joan was the giant's wife. Louise was the cow. Joseph was a guide at the top of the beanstalk who told Jack which way the castle was. Actors and actresses are quite temperamental, including my children. After three rehearsals, they all wanted to change parts, except nobody wanted to be the cow. I put up with all the noise for thirty minutes, then took down the curtain with great dramatics (it was probably my best performance) and canceled the play. They all cried, and that was that. Incidentally, I have lost the script.

I don't recall just how it happened, but one day Jackie and David managed to sneak off to Littlehampton, a seaside resort on the south coast of England. They weren't exactly alone; they took the fifteen children with them in our Ford wagon and David's Bedford van. Jackie later told me they shocked the local inhabitants as she and David strolled along the boardwalk. Jackie was carrying Ann. David was by her side. The fourteen other children, ranging in age from three to twelve years, were trailing along behind. A kindly lady, arrested by the sight, halted the group and said, "What lovely children. Is this a school?"

"Not altogether," said David. "These are our children."

"It's impossible," said the little old woman, as she started counting heads in serious fashion.

"I'm afraid it's true," replied David. "All these children belong to this sweet woman and myself. Bless her soul."

"I say it's impossible."

"Madam, it is not impossible. It has been done."

I later figured the situation out and came to the conclusion that it was indeed possible to have fifteen children in twelve years. It takes only 135 months to have fifteen children, and there are 144 months in twelve years. That leaves a full month between each. David had been quite correct.

By the spring of 1960, we had become attached to Dorking. We were the only Americans living there and had acquired quite a string of friends mostly through school and church connections. The townspeople grew accustomed to seeing our "green monster" station wagon cruise around, although a number of them thought the diplomat symbol CD on the rear bumper stood for "Civil Defense." We had adjusted to the local pattern of living and spent the better part of our Saturdays participating in that great social event known as shopping.

There were negative factors, however. The grind of commuting an hour and a half each way on buses, trains, and the subway was beginning to get me down. Moreover, we were required to attend a number of receptions, cocktail parties, and dinners in London. For most of these affairs, it meant that Jackie had to start getting dressed at three-thirty in the afternoon to catch a five o'clock train, and we would return home anywhere from eleven in the evening to one in the morning. Another consideration was that I periodically had the chore of being Duty Officer for the Embassy and had found it difficult on a number of emergency situations to get to the office in "five minutes." For these and a couple of other reasons, we started looking for a house in London. In May, when we learned that a US government-owned house in North London would be available in late fall, we applied and were accepted. It was a beautiful home in Hampstead Garden Suburb, perhaps the wealthiest area in all of England. We had additional good news: Jackie was expecting another English baby around the end of the year.

Chapter Seven

LIFE IN THE BIG CITY

We moved into our new home on December 20 and had all of four days to prepare for Christmas. The house was virtually the same size as the one in Dorking, but considerably more modern. It had a gas-fired central heating system that wouldn't quit. The garden was smaller, but adequate. The main second-story bathroom had a tub, a shower stall, a sink, and a bidet—everything but a toilet. I complained to the appropriate authorities and requested that the bidet be replaced by a toilet. I was told that the bidet had been there for fifteen years and that no one had ever objected to it before. The previous tenants had kept water lilies in it, and the ones before that had goldfish. I pointed out that there were ten persons in our family, that another would be arriving in a couple of weeks, and that a toilet would be far more functional in that bathroom than a goldfish bowl. We got the toilet. We also got television, which I had successfully managed to avoid in Dorking.

At 9:00 P.M. on January 7, 1961, Jackie said she was having pains ten minutes apart. "Sure," I said. "You and your false alarms. Let me know when they're thirty seconds apart."

"Okay," she said, "but they're pretty intense."

A half hour later she said, "They're three minutes apart."

"Into the car, quickly." We had seventeen miles to go. I tore across the North Circular Road and made it to Hangar Lane (about halfway) in twelve minutes.

"How much further?" she gasped. "I think I'm going to have it now."

"Don't be silly," I said. "We're almost there."

Five minutes and five miles later, "It's being born."

"For Pete's sake! Hold on, will you?"

"Malc, stop the car!"

"No." And I mashed down on the accelerator. Two minutes later, we were at the emergency entrance of the Ruislip Air Force Hospital. I leaped out of the car, grabbed an attendant by the arm, and said, "Quick. My wife is having a baby in the car."

"Relax," he said. "Take her to the Admission Office. It's just down the . . ."

"Are you kidding? This is our ninth."

"What?" And with that, he found a buddy and a stretcher within ten seconds. They snatched Jackie out of the car and disappeared down the corridor. I sat down in the waiting room, lit a cigarette, and opened a magazine. Before I finished reading the first ad, up came a doctor.

"Mr. Lawrence, you have a little girl. You didn't get here any too soon."

"Thanks, Doctor," I said and went in to see Jackie. They hadn't given her an anesthetic; there hadn't been time.

"Nice going, sweetheart. We made it," I said.

"Well, at least you didn't have to get somebody else to have the baby," she sighed.

"I'm glad," I said, kissing her on the cheek. We named the baby Ellen.

While Jackie and Ellen recovered, I found myself once again both father and mother to our brood for a week or so.

The age tally looked this way:

Theresa	thirteen and a half
Catherine	twelve and a half
Joan	eleven and a bit
Malcolm Jr.	nine and a third
Louise	eight and a bit
Joseph	six and a bit
Frances	three and a bit
Ann	fifteen months

We had taught them all but Ann how to wash, clean their teeth, and dress themselves. The older ones were even able to keep the living room straight and help in the kitchen. Everything went fine until I began to notice that Louise and Frances had terrible-looking hair. On my third morning as the little mother, I called them into the living room. I gathered Louise's long strands in my right hand, brushed them upward with my left, and asked her to turn around several times. When the whole business seemed to be tight enough, I jabbed in two bobby pins and reinforced the tuft with a rubber band. Frances was frightened to death and tried to run out of the house, but the older girls caught her. I did the same thing to her golden locks. I must say, when I finished, they did look lovely. That night, Louise and Fran asked me to take the rubber bands out so they could close their eyes.

The children made a nice transition to their new schools in London. The girls were enrolled in a convent school in Hendon, and the boys were sent to a Catholic lay school in Hampstead. Of course, everyone needed new uniforms, because the colors were different. We still have six brown uniforms from Dorking, going cheap if anyone is interested.

Foreign Service tours of duty overseas can be anywhere from two to six years, depending on the post and the individual concerned. The longer assignments are punctuated by a home leave trip to the United States after two or three years. This is to permit the Foreign Service officer and his family to keep in touch with things American and to allow the officer to have consultations with his superiors, end-users, and back-stoppers in the Department of State and other Washington agencies. My assignment to London worked out to a total of six years, with a home leave in the middle. The middle came up in July 1961.

As on our first crossing, we traveled by way of the SS *America*. The cruise was just as pleasant, except for a terrific storm that started up on the second day out. There was no pitch, but plenty of roll. By six o'clock, the rolling had built up to twenty-five to thirty degrees, and less than half of the passengers made it to the dining room. Ellen was tucked away in the stateroom with a bottle in her mouth, and we all progressed as far as the dining room door, but Joan lost her lunch at the entrance and went back to join the baby. The rest of us ate, almost.

By nine o'clock, the rolling action was up (or down) to thirty-five degrees, so we were told. At that hour, I was strolling on the Promenade Deck portside with an Embassy London colleague. As we turned into the lobby, we saw his wife in a sitting position sliding toward us. He reached down to assist her, and the ship rolled in the opposite direction. He fell, and they both went sliding on their backsides starboard bound. I glanced into the lounge and noticed that horse racing was on. It was the sixth race. The ship rolled, and every easy chair and its contents toppled over. Later that night, when Jackie and I had tied the kids to their bunks, we joined a small band of "die-hards" at the bar and stayed up until three in the morning catching drinks in our laps.

One day in mid-August, while I was lying on the beach at Bay Ridge, Maryland, re-Americanizing myself and watching the children drown each other, Jackie brought me a letter from my boss in London. It concerned the new emphasis being placed on the promotion of U.S. exports and inquired whether I would be willing to shift from economic work and become an Assistant Commercial Attaché. I rolled over, looked at Jackie, wrote "yes" in the sand, and followed up with a letter to London. Late in August, we sailed on the SS *United States* back to England and my new job.

From mid-1958 to mid-1961, my work at the London Embassy was as an Economic Defense Officer. The purpose of my job was to monitor and prevent unauthorized so-called East-West trade; that is, the shipment or transshipment of military equipment and other strategic U.S. products to East European countries or China. Working on tips from various sources, I investigated such illicit transactions, and if a British company was involved in these deals, I reported my findings to the Department of State and the Department of Commerce in Washington. U.S. Government sanctions were taken against U.S. and foreign companies deemed to be in violation of the law.

My work led to some interesting incidents. Some British firms would get wind of the fact that they were under investigation by the American Embassy. One day I received a visit to my office by a young female lawyer who was, to put it mildly, a "knockout." Dressed in a most sensual way, she attempted to convince me that the company she represented was not guilty of illegal transshipments of U.S. products. She had no substantive information, but was simply using her feminine wiles to get me to drop my investigation. She even offered me dinner and an evening "out." I declined her overtures and subsequently continued my investigation. As it turned out, the firm was guilty as suspected and was, in fact, suspended from trading in U.S. products for a number of years.

On another case involving a transshipment to a Communist bloc country, I received a telephone call from a woman with a most sultry voice possessing definite traces of an Eastern European accent. She invited me to have a drink after work at the Ritz Hotel in Piccadilly to discuss the case. Her big mistake was saying that I should meet her in the same spot we had had a drink earlier that year. I partook in no such meeting, but gave the details of our conversation to the appropriate authorities at the Embassy. Need I say that I had not had a drink with her "earlier that year."

From time to time, my name came up on the roster to be "duty officer" for the embassy during the night. One evening during one of my stints, I received a telephone call from a West End London pub owner informing me that a ranking U.S. military officer had left a briefcase under a table. He said he looked in the case to learn the owner's name, but saw only two things: an electric razor and a thick packet of papers marked "Top Secret."

I drove to the pub immediately, retrieved the briefcase, and delivered it to the Marine guard at the Embassy. The guard informed me the next day that the officer in question called on the Embassy and said he was looking for a lost briefcase that contained his electric razor and wondered if anyone had turned it in. The officer was subsequently "busted" and relieved of his duties in London.

On another occasion when I was duty officer, a woman called me from a fashionable London hotel to report that her husband had just made love to her and that he was dying. I gave her the name of a doctor. She called me back later to say that her husband did not die. I thanked her for the call.

On the top front of the new American Embassy building, which opened in 1959, was a huge gold eagle that was criticized by some Britishers as being too gaudy for Grosvenor Square. Late one night—again as duty officer—I received a call from an irate individual who said he detested the eagle. He wanted it taken down the next day or he would remove it himself. The man was obviously inebriated, but I reported the call to security anyway.

It might seem that Jackie had done little else during our first three years in England than have babies and take care of the house. This is far from the truth. She had domestic help and devoted a great deal of her time to such annual charity events as the Kensington Spring Fair, the English Speaking Union International Bazaar, the American Women's Club Charity Bazaar, and the Christmas Party for the Benefit of Needy Children. She had, moreover, worked on the annual Spring Fair in Dorking and a number of other benefits for the local churches and schools.

After our return to England, she took on an additional little project; she joined the American Embassy Wives' Speakers Bureau, a small group of brave women who traveled the countryside delivering talks to local women's organizations. Jackie's first speaking assignment, so she was told, was to be with a small group of Gas Federation Wives in Ealing. The set-up was that she would sit with a group of eight to ten ladies and chat over a cup of tea about the American way of life. Despite the apparent informal flavor of the meeting, this was to be Jackie's first effort, and she prepared a fairly comprehensive address.

It was a good thing, too. She arrived at the appointed place, opened the door, and saw a crowd of some 150 women seated on either side of an aisle leading to a stage. The president of the organization greeted Jackie, led her up onto the stage, and left her standing there alone, without a stick of furniture. Her heart was in her mouth. Realizing that she would look silly standing on the bare stage reading her address, Jackie rolled up the sheets of paper, held them behind her and delivered her talk extemporaneously. She received much applause and a cup of tea for her efforts. After that it was easy. Subsequent assignments took her to Tunbridge Wells, Newbury, Salisbury, Bath, and other points of interest.

By mid-fall the social season was again in full swing. Until something different is invented, I suppose cocktail parties will go on as an essential feature of diplomatic life. After more than three years in England, we had had our share of that form of socializing and had begun to get more of it with my assignment in commercial work. We did make many friends at these affairs, and I found the cocktail party a useful means for establishing worthwhile business contacts. However, the conversations were pretty superficial at times. I recall one with, let us say, a Mrs. Smith that went something like this:

> "Hello, Mrs. Smith. How are you?" I inquired.
>
> "Oh. Hello there. I'm fine, thank you. And how are you?"
>
> "Fine, thanks," I commented brightly. At that point, there was a fairly long pause during which both Mrs. Smith and I tried frantically to think of something really intelligent to say. Finally, I blurted out with, "Horrible weather we're having, isn't it?"
>
> "Oh, I think it's so-so for this time of year, don't you?"
>
> "Yes, I suppose so. Are you from London?" I asked.
>
> "Oh, yes," she said, looking for someplace to flick an inch of ashes.
>
> "Where?"
>
> "Where what?" she asked.
>
> "In which section of London do you currently reside?"
>
> "Oh! We live in Seven Oaks."
>
> "But Seven Oaks is in Kent, not London," I pointed out.
>
> "Oh, you're quite right. How silly of me. What did you say your name was?"
>
> "Lawrence. I'm with the American Embassy. I've been . . ."
>
> "Oh, then you're the husband of that lovely Mrs. Lawrence, the one with the nine children. I don't know how

she does it. I mean, stay so young and slim. Are there any twins?"

"Yes, I'm her husband. No, there are no twins. We did it the hard way. Heh, heh."

"Oh, I think it's amazing. She could be one of your daughters."

"Thank you very much, but I don't think her mother would understand."

"Oh, I must introduce you to my husband. He's the Managing Director of _____ Bank, you know."

"No, I didn't know, but I'd be delighted to meet him anyway."

"Oh, you funny boy, you. Come along."

And so, I met Mr. Smith, and he became a most worthwhile contact. I really didn't resent Mrs. Smith or all of the other Mrs. Smiths I met at these cocktail parties, but after a while, Jackie and I became known primarily as the parents of nine children. We were proud of our kids, but hoped that people would see something else in us besides the fact that we had been able to go through the physical exercise of having nine offspring. One very bad joke thrown at us was, "You can prevent that sort of thing with orange juice, you know."

"Orange juice? Before or after?" I inquired.

"Instead, old boy, instead. Wah, hah, hah, hah."

At any rate, Jackie and I decided that rather than have the news of nine children (for whatever that was worth) go buzzing around cocktail parties, we would take the offensive and begin questioning our new acquaintances on the status of their families. That way, they would be forced to talk about themselves, and then maybe people would begin to recognize our other fine talents (which I won't go into here).

We put our new tactic into play at a large reception at Grosvenor House, a posh hotel on Park Lane. As was our custom (so to mix better), Jackie and I separated after the first five minutes. I wandered around with a drink in one hand and a cigarette in the other, engaging myself in a number of brief but enlightening conversations with several of my friends. Ultimately, I was introduced to a Mrs. Jones, who likewise was endowed with a glass and a cigarette.

"It's a pleasure to meet you, Mrs. Jones. Are you married?"

"Really, Mr. Lawrence. That's a frightfully forward question."

"Don't get me wrong, Mrs. Jones. I was just making conversation. Are you married, incidentally?"

"Well . . . yes, I am," she replied, spilling her ashes on the forty thousand dollar rug.

"Do you have any children?" I inquired.

"I really don't see how that's any of your . . ."

"Please! Just answer the question, Mrs. Jones."

"Why . . . I—I have five children, three boys and two girls," she said, as her cigarette fell into her highball.

"WHAT??? FIVE CHILDREN???" I bellowed. "Why on earth did you have five children? Don't you realize that the population explosion is bad enough without people in civilized countries trying to see how many kids they can have? With all the uncertainty in the world today, I really can't see how anyone could have the nerve or the conscience to bring five innocent, helpless human beings into this miserable maelstrom."

"Well! I've never been so insulted in my . . ."

"I haven't finished yet, Mrs. Jones," I said.

"But I have, with you," she said and walked off in a huff.

I looked around for someone else with whom to strike up an acquaintanceship. About twenty minutes later, I bumped into Jackie. "How are you doing, Jacq?" I asked.

"Well," she said, "about ten minutes ago, I was standing over there talking with a few of the girls. I was introduced to a Mrs. Jones. We started discussing children, and someone mentioned that I had nine. This Mrs. Jones grabbed me by the arm and told me for God's sake not to go near the rude man who was going around insulting everybody with children. Someone asked Mrs. Jones where the man was, and she pointed you out. We all had a good laugh, but Mrs. Jones just walked away."

"Don't worry about it, Jacq," I said. "She did the exact same thing to me. She must be some kind of a crank."

"Are you sure you're not carrying your new offensive tactics too far, dear?" Jackie asked.

Big families call for pictures. I'm no photography bug. In fact, I have never owned a decent camera. Over the years, however, we managed to collect thousands of photographs of the kids doing one thing or another. Each time I would take a couple of rolls of film, the family could hardly wait to see them. It has always been a big occasion when I walk in the door and say, "Kids, the pictures are here." The children would charge me, grab the envelope, and spend the next thirty minutes (it took that long) passing the prints around. Within the next day or so, the pictures would gravitate to one of the large cardboard cartons containing hundreds of earlier images and rest there untouched until they were rediscovered years later. We never put dates on the photographs, so there are always heated arguments during the rediscovery periods as to when and where the things were taken.

The photographic record of the Lawrence family is not a completely slipshod affair, however. I have insisted on a formal portrait every five years, right on schedule in order that each person could be properly identified by both name and age. It started with a marriage portrait of Jackie and myself in 1946. By 1951, Theresa, Catherine, Joan, and Malcolm had arrived on the scene. In 1956, Louise and Joseph completed the picture.

Christmas of 1961 was rolling around, and it was time for another one of the stellar productions. I was a little worried that the others would resent being squeezed together to make room in front of the camera for Frances, Ann, and Ellen. The household was quite a scene that Saturday morning early in December. The photographer was coming at eleven o'clock, and for two hours beforehand Jackie was trying to hold down the number of dresses the girls were pulling out of their closets, trying on, and throwing on the floor. It was simple for the two boys and me: we had only one suit apiece. By eleven, for the first time in five years, everyone looked decent at the same time. The photographer was prompt, and we assembled in the living room. We posed on the semi-circular seat inside the large bay window. The camera began clicking away.

After several shots, Jackie said, "Wait a minute. Where's Ann?" Ann was missing. Everybody screamed for two-year-old Ann. "Mommy!" Ann called from the top of the landing, and fell all the way down the stairs. She was a well-padded child and managed to escape with only one minor injury—but oh, where that was. She had scraped all the skin off the front of her nose, perhaps the most important part of the anatomy as far as photographs are concerned. We doctored up that little thing with a variety of skin-colored salves and powder. At last she was as good as new, and the eleven of us took up our positions on the window seat. The little man started again with the camera. Twenty-five shots he took. On the following Wednesday he telephoned Jackie to say that his lens had been faulty and asked if he could come back the next week. Needless to say the pictures that were taken the following Saturday contained a minimum of smiles.

By the spring of 1962, Ellen was a walker, and the whole family began spending pleasant Sunday afternoons exploring our neighborhood. Hampstead Garden Suburb originated in the late 1920s as a housing area for middle-class working families with row houses and duplexes. During the 1930s, as construction spread eastward, the new houses became larger and larger, and by World War II, the suburb had developed into a place where money lived, with fabulous mansions on Winnington Road and Bishop's Avenue (Millionaire's Row). Our house, a detached structure then worth about $75,000, was in the middle of the two sections with respect to both location and value. We were within a mile of Hampstead, an uptown village noted for its arty set, with such famous places as the Old Bull and Bush, Spaniard's Inn, Jack Straw's Castle, Keat's House, Golders Hill Park, and the stately Kenwood House with its art collection and magnificent grounds. Our favorite haunt, though, was the Hampstead Heath, a rolling mixture of trees and fields. The high point of the Heath was Parliament Hill, which looked out over much of London and was the ideal spot for the March and April kite fliers. We joined the set that season with our kite and two thousand feet of string.

We normally ended our Sunday outings around four o'clock, passing on foot through Spaniard's Gate into our suburb, the land of Rolls-Royces, Bentleys, Jaguars, and a 1954 Ford station wagon. After a relaxing drink on the patio, we would have a delicious meal and, during coffee, gaze through the French windows and watch the birds in our garden prepare for bed. On one such evening, I commented to Jackie, "It's difficult to believe that the leisurely life of Hampstead could exist inside the second-largest city in the world."

"I know," she said. "It's so completely different from the rest of London—like a fairy-tale kingdom."

"That reminds me. We have an invitation to a garden party at Buckingham Palace."

"How thrilling, Malc. Is it from the Queen?"

"No, but it's almost as good; the Lord Chamberlain was commanded by Her Majesty to invite us."

"Oh! Can we go?"

"I don't know. We were just over at their place in November 1958, and we haven't returned the invitation," I said.

"Don't stand on ceremony. They weren't expecting an invite from us. Can we go?"

"Well, I guess so. It will be nice, and I suppose we really should keep up the contact."

"Oh, I knew you would say yes," she said. A couple of days later, she went into the West End and bought a pink outfit with a white flowered hat. I had a special place to acquire my garments on a rental basis.

The event took place on a wonderfully warm day late in July. After lunch, Jackie and I dressed and paraded ourselves in the garden before the children. Our next-door neighbors came over to find out what was happening.

"Where on earth are you going dressed like that?" the better-half inquired.

"Malcolm and I have been invited to have tea with the Queen in the garden of Buckingham Palace," Jackie said.

"With the Queen? How wonderful! We've never even seen her before, up close, that is. Do tell us all about it when you return," said our neighbor.

"The last time we were there, it was inside the palace, and we had cocktails and danced," I chimed in. "It will be grand seeing Phil and the gang again."

We returned home about seven. The neighbors raced over.

"Tell us. How was it? Who was there?" they asked.

"It was terrific," I said. "Truly delightful. The Queen was there and, let's see, oh yes, Prince Philip. And then, of course, Jacqueline and myself and about 2,700 other people. It was most cozy."

In large families, it is convenient, if not essential, to establish and maintain certain household routines. There should be a time to rise, a time to eat, a time to work, a time to play, etc. The collective or "togetherness" approach also extends perforce to family outings, vacations, watching television, parlor games, and other forms of amusement. The parents attempt to strike a happy medium between the younger and older children and, in the process, play toward the middle. This sort of thing can be fairly easy when the children are small, but as the number increases, so does the spread in age, and it becomes more and more difficult to find common denominators.

By the fall of 1962, Jackie and I fully realized that our fifteen-year old enjoyed very few of the things that the one-year-old baby did. They both liked to eat and sleep, of course, but not necessarily at the same times. While Theresa enjoyed playing with Ellen, she quickly grew tired of shaking a rattle in her face, and Ellen, on the other hand, really didn't go too much for rock and roll records. Something in the middle, like a bow and arrow set, would only interest Joseph, who was eight at the time.

It was at that point that a natural division occurred among our children, consisting of the "teenagers" (Theresa, Catherine, and Joan), the "middle group" (Malcolm, Louise, and Joseph), and the "babies" (Frances, Ann, and Ellen). Common interests were nourished within each group, and for us it was like having three little families instead of one big one. This development made it easier for us sociologically but not physically. Unless one sets up some kind of a domestic work camp, I simply do not agree with those many people who have commented to us, "It's much easier with a large family; the children take care of each other." They may "take care" of each other on occasion, but it's usually with their fists and not by doing the laundry.

However, with the advent of the teenager group, we did have some pretty good built-in baby-sitters who saved us some money. After a while though, it started working in reverse and we got this argument: "Okay, Mom," Theresa said one Friday morning, "we sat with the kids on Monday and Wednesday when you and Dad went to those parties. Tomorrow night, there's a dance at the church. Catherine, Joan, and I want to go, and you two will have to baby-sit."

"But Theresa," Jackie said, "Joan is only thirteen."

"So what? She looks sixteen. Besides, we'll take care of her."

"How much do we get?" I asked.

"For what?" Theresa asked.

"For baby-sitting." And so, they started going to the weekly Teen Club dances, and we had lost our baby-sitters for at least one night a week.

One sunny morning in early June 1963, Theresa came down late for breakfast. She said she felt weak and dizzy and was having difficulty swallowing. I recalled that she had had sneezing attacks for two or three days and thought she was suffering from some sort of allergy. We decided to keep her home that day and sent the other children off to school. Jackie asked Theresa to lie on the couch and fixed her a cup of tea. As Theresa sipped the tea, it came out of her nose. She couldn't swallow at all. Moreover, at that point she admitted that she saw everything double. She got up and tried to walk, but her legs wouldn't work. A moment later, her speech failed. These symptoms were completely new to us. I carried Theresa to the car, and the three of us headed for the U.S. Navy Dispensary in downtown London.

The car had overheated on a number of occasions and it did so again that morning in the midst of a monumental traffic jam just three blocks shy of the dispensary. Jackie and Theresa transferred into a taxi, and I remained literally in the middle of the street faced with the task of making the car disappear. I finally managed to have it towed away and reached the dispensary around nine o'clock. Jackie and Theresa had already departed in an ambulance for the Air Force Hospital in Ruislip. The dispensary physician informed me that Theresa had one of three things: meningitis, bulbar polio, or a rare virus known as Guillain-

Barré's Disease, a paralysis which attacks the upper respiratory and involuntary nervous systems.

I went to the Embassy and tried desperately to contact Jackie by telephone. When I connected shortly after ten o'clock, she told me that Theresa's case had been diagnosed as Guillain-Barré's Disease, that she was in the midst of a forty-eight-hour crisis period, that the illness was often fatal, and that the hospital chaplain was at the moment giving Theresa the sacrament of extreme unction. Our first child was in danger of dying.

The hospital room that afternoon was an eerie sight for parents. It was much worse for the patient, a frightened girl on the eve of her sixteenth birthday. On one side of her bed was an oxygen tent, and on the other, equipment set up for a tracheotomy. The doctor had explained to Theresa the nature and seriousness of her condition because her cooperation would be an essential factor in conquering the crisis. Panic and fear would close up her throat, and if not lead to death, would in any event call for surgery—and even surgery was no guaranteed cure. No medication was prescribed. For some cases cortisone had been used, but a minority of the patients pulled through. And so, we all had to wait, especially Theresa.

Theresa, a beautiful blue-eyed child with long blond hair—who at eighteen months of age had darted away from me out of the park into heavy traffic and was saved by some fast running on my part, who at age two had learned by heart all of the words to the songs I sang in the band, who for years had been "big sister" to all the little ones who followed her, who had been my constant companion on shopping tours, who had done well in school, who by fifteen had read more books than anyone else her age we knew, who had become a most devout Catholic—now lay in a hospital bed with eyes wide open, realizing that her time may have come. The long hours passed slowly. She barely slept at all;

and neither did Jackie, who for forty hours kept the vigil at Theresa's side.

On June 4 the crisis was over, and Theresa smiled. She had been saved by five doctors, nurses around the clock, and her mother. More than that; she had saved herself, with her inner calm, her courage, and her determination to live. Pope John XXIII had died the day before. When we told her this, she commented that everyone in heaven had been so busy with arrangements for him, there hadn't been time for her. Theresa's recovery was miraculous. She was out of the hospital in two weeks, on her feet ten days later, and completely recovered by mid-summer. Jackie and I had experienced our first major family crisis, which most fortunately ended happily.

One bright spot we did enjoy in 1963 was the news that Jackie and I were asked to represent the American Embassy at the London premiere of the motion picture *The V.I.Ps,* featuring Elizabeth Taylor and Richard Burton. At the appointed hour, we approached the entrance to a West End theater in a long black limousine. Floodlights were playing all about the area, and hundreds of people were gathered at the scene in hopes of spotting Taylor and Burton and the other celebrities as they pulled up to the marquee. When our limousine reached that spot, several fans looked into our windows on both sides. One yelled out, "Who is it?" Another replied, "Nobody." Despite that put-down, we exited the car gracefully, entered the theater with great aplomb, and thoroughly enjoyed the show. Afterwards, Jackie asked me, "Just who are you anyway?" I answered, "Nobody."

In the fall of 1963, motorcycles and hot-rods began appearing at our front door. Strange-looking people with long hair and leather jackets edged their way into our living room. (Of course, my thick hair and zoot suit in the 1940s had been an entirely different thing, I told myself.) Jackie and I listened to the various stories about the "Mods" and "Rockers"; there was a real war on between those two groups, and we didn't quite appreciate the significance of it all. What was happening to the world? We were just growing old, we guessed.

Before long, the Twist and Beatlemania hit our household. I assured Jackie that both the dance and the Beatles were fads which would run their course in less than a year. My main objection to the Twist was that I couldn't do it very well. I resented the Beatles because they made the girls cry. Our three oldest girls liked that sort of thing, however, and even sneaked out of the house at 2:00 A.M. one morning and, along with thousands of other girls, went to London Airport to welcome the Beatles back from their tour in the United States. A week or so later, the motorcycle boys escorted my car carrying Theresa, Catherine, and Joan to a live Beatles concert at a nearby Odeon theater where they enjoyed front row seats. When I picked them up after the show, there were tears in their eyes. They told me that everybody was screaming and crying. Imagine!

Jackie and I devoted most of our spare time in those days learning to form and/or tolerate the teenage mind. We found it a stimulating experience and a mental challenge. It was at last our time to be pigeon-holed as squares, people aloof and apart who had never been young and who lacked any degree of understanding as to what life was all about. Such people, naturally, were only concerned with money, impressions they made on others, taking care of the house, and—above all—keeping teenagers tied down, hemmed in, and generally stifled. "Imagine, Malc," Jackie said one evening when the house was quiet and we were into a drink, "with six more coming along, we're going to have this teenage business for another seventeen years."

"I think that will be just great—for them," I said. I drained my glass, walked over to the music "coffin," and put on an old Benny Goodman record. I turned the volume up, real loud.

"Solid, man! Let's dance," I entreated Jackie.

"I prefer Glenn Miller," she replied.

Our days in England were numbered. We regretted the prospect of leaving the London theater, the walks in Hampstead Heath, the trips to the south coast, the visits to museums and stately homes, the cruises up the Thames, the English pubs, and, most of all, the many good friends we had made—both English and American—during our six years. However, we counted our blessings when we learned that following another home leave in the States, our next assignment would be Bern, Switzerland. We were further heartened by the news that I had received another promotion.

Early one morning in July 1964, we waved good-bye to our friends and neighbors in Hampstead Garden Suburb, climbed into three London taxis, and made our way to the airport to catch a Boeing 707 destined for the United States.

Chapter Eight

AH, SWITZERLAND

Switzerland is a nation possessed not only of mountains, watches, cheese, chocolates, and yodelers, but of precision instruments, generators, marine engines, chemicals and pharmaceuticals, financial wizardry, and neutrality.

As a citizen of the United States having resided in Switzerland, it is only fitting that I point out some of the basic differences between the two countries. In the first place, Switzerland is smaller than the United States. With an area of sixteen thousand square miles, it could fit three times in the state of New York. For a variety of reasons, the Swiss have not attempted this feat even once. Switzerland compensates for its smaller size with a longer history. The Swiss Confederation was founded by the three Forest Cantons in 1291, some 485 years before the American Colonies got together. But we come out on top in population, with 281 million compared with 7.3 million. The Swiss retaliate with four national languages (German, French, Italian, and Romansch) as opposed to our one.

Moreover, a great percentage of the Swiss speak our language, and I would estimate that English is second only to German for the country as a whole.

Perhaps the most significant difference between the two countries relates to eggs. In the United States, the vast majority of eggs have centrally-located yolks. In Switzerland most eggs are laid on mountains, and the yolks are either at the top or the bottom of the shells depending on which direction the hens are facing.

The people are different too. To the Swiss—thanks to television and motion pictures—the typical American male has lots of money, two automobiles, has had three wives, and is constantly being shot at in the streets by other Americans. When seen abroad, he sports a camera and a wife with a mink coat. The typical Swiss male, on the other hand, lives on a mountain, smokes a pipe, carries a stick, and invariably has a daughter named Heidi. He is usually eating cheese and chocolates at the same time.

Following a pleasant six weeks in the United States, we arrived in Zurich by air on August 17 and took the train to Bern. We were installed in three apartments in the Silvahof Hotel, which is located just next door to the American Embassy on the bank of the swift-flowing Aare River. Finding a suitable house proved to be considerably more difficult than in England. We were to stay at the Silvahof a full three months. As it turned out, only one house turned up. It had six bedrooms, and we took it.

In the meantime, we settled into our new country of assignment from the hotel. We enrolled the three older girls in the Pensionnat International de la Chassotte, a Catholic boarding and day school for girls in Fribourg, a French-speaking city twenty miles south of Bern. The girls started their own little grind of commuting by train and had the double treat of receiving all instructions in the French language (imagine taking English grammar in French). Malcolm Jr. commuted to Fribourg too, but attended the Villa St. Jean, a boys' school run by an American Catholic teaching order. Louise, Joseph, Frances, and Ann were placed in the English Speaking School of Bern (Whoever heard of a school speaking?). Ellen was only three and a half and had another year to wait; Jackie did the best she could to make a home out of three apartments. I had a job to do, of course, and set off each morning on a forty-yard march to the Embassy.

My new position carried the title of Commercial Attaché. This was clearly the most interesting and responsible assignment so far. I was beginning my fifteenth year with the Department of State and felt grateful that I had selected foreign service as my vocation. During my first eight years with the Department, I was charged with writing intelligence research reports on the economies of France, Belgium, the Netherlands, and Luxembourg. The job permitted me to sharpen my academic tools and to gain an insight into European industrial, commercial, and financial developments and all phases of economic policies and practices.

I was then shifted to more of an "action" job for my assignment in London when I served as a so-called Economic Defense Officer, with duties relating primarily to the enforcement of U.S. export control regulations. The move into commercial work at London led to a broader range of duties. It is one of the larger embassies, of course; and there were several commercial officers, each with responsibilities for a defined group of economic sectors. Within our areas, we were designated as "action officers" for all aspects of commercial work and export promotion, including trade, correspondence, market research, trade missions, trade exhibitions, congressional delegations, speeches, plant visits, and you name it—we did it.

With one-eighth the population, Switzerland is less important than the United Kingdom as a market for U.S. exports, but the commercial program is of the same intensity, and the position of the Commercial Attaché carries with it, under the direction of the Ambassador, the function of coordinating all aspects of United States commercial policy for the country as a whole. I was thus happy with my new job in Bern and set about my duties with great vigor and determination.

I bought a new Volkswagon minibus, which seemed to be the only thing available that would come close to holding all of us. I had sold the "green monster" in England to—of all people—the rag and bone man (junkman). Actually, no one else had made me an offer. The car had developed a rather nasty leak in the automatic transmission (about a quart a week) and, among other things, had caught on fire two or three times.

On November 20, we bid farewell to the Silvahof and moved into our new home on Effingerstrasse in the heart of Bern. A three-story townhouse with a full basement, it was situated on a quiet private street in the middle of a row of thirteen almost identical houses built in the late nineteenth century. The houses had a mews-type setting with the entrances on the "back street" and small gardens "out front" facing the main thoroughfare. Our household effects arrived in good time, and we found a place for everything.

There was only one problem: our prized double bed frame was damaged beyond repair. The boxspring and mattress were okay and served as a makeshift bed for Jackie and me. But it wasn't long before she started complaining about sleeping "practically on the floor." After much discussion (mostly about money), we decided that it would be more sensible for me to try my hand at building a bed rather than buy a new one. So I bought some lumber and proceeded with my new do-it-yourself assignment. For some reason (probably because I didn't own a jigsaw), the headboard turned out square. It was five feet wide and, when assembled, stood three feet above the mattress. It looked very plain and amateurish indeed. I painted it, but that didn't help much. "I know," I said one evening to Jackie. "I'll mount a big glass mirror on it."

"But, Malc," she said. "What would our friends say? You know what I mean; a thing like that on our bed would be most unusual."

"So what? We don't sleep on the bed when our friends are in the room. Besides, it's a nice conversation piece and will give the gals something to talk about when they come up to powder their noses. Maybe their husbands will make new beds for them."

"Okay, if you think it will look nice," she said.

"Sure it will. Heh, heh."

So I mounted the mirror, and it looked great. When our friends saw it, they either raised their eyebrows or cleared their throats. Nobody ever said anything about it. One thing though: it made our bedroom look bigger.

Our neighbors were solid Bernese who had lived on Effingerstrasse for years and years. Most of them were considerably senior to us in age. We were not only the first strangers to move into the neighborhood for a decade or so, but we were "foreign" strangers. Nevertheless, we quickly became friendly with the people on either side, and our absorption into the neighborhood became complete with our participation in the "longest-day party," a traditional celebration held every June 21.

As far as I know, there is no party quite like it anywhere else in Bern, and as newcomers we were flattered by the invitation. It's a picnic held literally in the middle of the street, complete with decorative flags and lanterns. Everyone contributes food and drink, and the thing gets under way with about forty-five people at 6:00 P.M. The children disappear by midnight, and the old folks continue on with liquid refreshments, chatting and relating stories in several languages. My French always becomes better at times like that. By 4:00 A.M. everyone is in bed whether he's tired or not. The Swiss are hard to beat. The morning after our first party, I made the supreme effort of getting up at nine o'clock to help clean the street. I looked out of the window; it had all been done.

Toward the end of the party, I had had a conversation with the neighbor on our left, a lovely lady whose husband was a doctor. I think it went like this: "Hey, Mr. Lawrence, have you had the pleasure of Isenfluh?"

"Hey!" I responded, clinking her glass. "I have had several types of flu, but never the Isenflu. What are the symptoms?"

"You are so silly, you Americans. Isenfluh is a fine place in the Bernese Oberland near Lauterbrunnen; it is a small willage (village). Swiss school children have built the road to Isenfluh with their bare hands."

"In the first place," I said, "all Americans aren't silly. In the second place, I hate to think of driving along a road built out of childrens' hands. I have children of my own, you know."

"Mr. Lawrence, try not to be funny. You go some day where I have told you, and you will be happy there."

"I certainly am looking for some place to be happy, Madam," I said.

The next Sunday morning I woke up early. I rolled over in bed, an action which pulled the covers off of Jackie. I gazed at her figure, reclining in the shape of an "S." I said, "Hey, Jacq, what about Isenfluh?"

"What about him?"

"It's not a him; it's a place highly recommended to me the other night by one of our neighbors. I forgot to tell you. It's supposed to be better than the Jungfraujoch, the Matterhorn, and the Bear Pits in Bern, even."

"If you fix breakfast, I'll go anywhere with you," she sighed.

"It isn't our second honeymoon, you know. The kids are going with us."

"Of all the things I need now," she commented, "a second honeymoon isn't one of them."

"Good," I yelped and leapt out of bed to prepare a simple breakfast for eleven.

It was noon when we reached Lauterbrunnen, a resort village halfway up the Alps to such other resort villages as Wengen and Murren. Near the mountain train station, we took a right turn onto the road to Isenfluh. At the foot of the climb, there was a sign with a lot of German words written on it. I assumed it told all about the childrens' hands, but having already heard the story, I didn't bother to read it and proceeded upward. After several hundred yards, the road narrowed down to what appeared to be a six-foot width, or approximately two inches wider than the minibus. I noticed—but Jackie observed with even greater interest because the view was on her side—that there was no protective railing on the road. Her attention was drawn even more to the sheer drop of five hundred, then one thousand feet.

"Spectacular," I announced. "I wonder what would happen if we should meet a car coming down the mountain? I suppose one of us would have to back up—or down. Or maybe one of us could turn around." I told Jackie not to lean against the door because it had a tricky catch. My advice was hardly necessary, however, as she was practically sitting in my lap and staring with breathless admiration at the beautiful view. This time, she wasn't crimson, but green. The children were happy in the rear two seats of the minibus, wrestling and commenting on how sensational it would be if we should suddenly go off the edge of the mountain.

We rode to the end of the road, parked the bus, gathered the picnic equipment, and entered a thick woods. I found a narrow path and penetrated the woods, deeper and deeper. Some of the children were blazing their own trails on either side of us. After about fifteen minutes, we heard Joseph shout that he and

Malcolm had discovered a good eating place. Then we heard Frances exclaim that she had found something else.

"Look, Mommy, Daddy! Come here, quick!" she screamed.

"Okay, Fran," I puffed. "Don't get excited. We're coming." Everyone ran to where Frances was spreading some bushes apart. There it was: a perpendicular drop of at least one thousand feet. We peered below at an inch-square gas station and several minute objects moving like automobiles. Up to that time, Malcolm and Joseph had been dashing madly through the trees and bushes making like Robin Hood and his men. For an obvious reason, they had to stop that little game. We backed up thirty yards, spread the picnic blanket, and enjoyed our peanut butter, cheese, and jelly sandwiches.

The trip down the mountain was the same as the trip up, except the view was on my side. Despite my earlier request, Jackie was leaning against the door with the tricky catch, a factor which may well have kept us from going off the mountain. When we reached the bottom, I got out of the bus and attempted to read what was written on that sign. What it said, in effect, was that traffic was to move up the mountain during even hours and down during odd hours—or maybe it was the other way around. Whatever it was, fortune had been on our side. I had unwittingly negotiated the mountain at the correct times. When I later asked my neighbor why she hadn't told me about the hours and the steep drop in the woods, she replied, "You did not ask."

Isenfluh had been nice, but we looked for even greener pastures that summer. Early one morning in August, we crammed the family and six suitcases into the minibus and set off for a week's holiday on the French Riviera. Our route was Geneva, Grenoble, Gap, Digne, Grasse, Nice, then to an apartment in Beaulieu-sur-Mer. It was a picturesque but grueling trip, mostly through rugged mountainous areas. We got to know each other quite well after that fourteen-hour, practically non-stop drive. It was worth it though. We had a truly delightful week: Cannes for swimming and sunning, Nice for strolling and eating, and Monte Carlo for the Palace and the Casino (I lost). And, of course, we did the Cornishes by minibus. Our return trip to Switzerland by way of the Maritime Alps, Turin, and the Great St. Bernard Pass was no less grueling, but by far the more spectacular route.

The Riviera trip was planned as a special treat for the family prior to the departure of Theresa, Catherine, and Joan, who were being sent "away" to school in September. Theresa was registered as a freshman at the University of Maryland Extension School in Munich, Germany. To provide Catherine and Joan with a transition into the American system of education, we enrolled them in a U.S. Air Force high school at Dreux, France, a small town located about fifty miles west of Paris.

In actual fact, the girls weren't sent to school. Not wanting my driving skills to become rusty, I drove them. Late in August, the minibus was loaded with the three girls, all of their earthly possessions, and Malcolm Jr. as my navigator. The scene in front of our house was but one of three displays of emotion that occurred on that famous trip. The time was 3:30 A.M. Swarming around the minibus, all dressed in their night garments, were Jackie, Louise, Joseph, Frances, Ann, and Ellen. It was dark, but not too dark to see unhappiness on eleven faces, mine included, as I pretended to busy myself with the last-minute check on gas, lights, luggage, and the coffee thermos.

"Don't forget to write," said Jackie. "And be good girls. Do you hear? And telephone if you get into any kind of trouble. Do you hear?" Louise and Fran seemed to have something in their eyes. The throats in the minibus began to swell. At that point, everyone looked in different directions, clamped eyes, and wiped away signs of sorrows. After twenty-two kisses and two handshakes, someone yelled, "Good-bye, stupid." With that, I put the bus in first gear, simultaneously released the clutch and compressed the accelerator, and drove from Bern to Munich to Dreux to Bern—thirteen hundred miles. I had to stop a couple of times, of course, and the trip took three days.

On the last leg of the journey, Malcolm and I woke up at seven o'clock in the morning after a three-hour nap in the bus, which was parked beneath a castle wall in Langres, France. There, we recounted the highlights of the trip.

"What time do you think we'll get to Bern?" he asked.

"I would imagine about 10:30. Why?"

"Because I have it all figured out," he said. "If we get home by then, the whole trip will take seventy-nine hours. According to my count, you will have driven for thirty-nine hours or almost one-half of the time. You said the trip was 2,200 kilometers. That is 1,320 miles. So our average speed will be 33.8 miles per hour. That isn't very fast."

"I thought it would be closer to thirty-five. Still, it's faster than by horseback," I commented.

"Theresa looked pretty sad when we left her in front of the dorm," Malcolm offered. "But she didn't cry."

"That's what you think. Anyway, she'll manage. She is eighteen, after all."

"Yeah. It was too bad about Catherine. She threw up all the way across France."

"Yes. I told her not to drink that pint of chocolate milk after the three cheeseburgers at the snackbar."

"How about her getting sick right in the middle of the public square in Strasbourg," he said.

"It was even better," I pointed out, "when she did it just in front of the large picture window at that French restaurant."

"Yeah, but I guess she couldn't help it."

"I suppose not. Otherwise, I'm sure she wouldn't have done it again while we were visiting the Eiffel Tower."

"I felt so sorry for Catherine and Joan last night when we left them just standing out there in the middle of the street. They didn't even have a room yet. They were both crying."

"I know," I replied. "I couldn't see so well myself at the time. But I suppose it made them feel much better when I yelled out of the car window for them not to worry about it."

"Yeah," he said. "I guess you can get used to anything after a while."

"Almost anything," I replied. "I'm not so sure I could spend the rest of my life behind this wheel. I thought I had had it last night, driving for six hours against the glaring headlights of all those cars heading back to Paris. I always knew Paris was deserted for the month of August, but I didn't realize that everyone went south."

"You look tired, Pop. What are you going to do when we get home?" Malcolm asked.

"Are you kidding? I'm going to run around the block sixteen times and then take what's left of the family for a long drive in the country."

"Sure," he said.

I drained my coffee cup, lit a cigarette, and pressed on toward Bern.

★ *Chapter Nine* ★

THE JOYS OF COMMUNITY PROJECTS

An important part of the job of representing one's country overseas is participation in community affairs. One doesn't necessarily have to be a do-gooder and run around looking for projects. Good causes have fairly long and strong tentacles which have a way of finding people and placing them on teams. The decent thing, I suppose, is for one to do whatever one can when called on and thus avoid the reputation of being a do-nothing. The tentacles have been successful in reaching out and grabbing Jackie and me on the odd occasion.

One morning in March 1965 as I sat in my office vigorously making plans for participation by U.S. industry in a Swiss international trade exhibition, an Embassy associate walked in and sank down into an easy chair facing my desk.

"Hi, Malcolm," he said. "How are you?"

"I'm fine, thanks. And you?"

"Oh, I'm fine, thanks. You keeping busy?"

"You bet," I said, wondering if this was a courtesy call or a rehearsal for a cocktail party.

"You have some children in the school, don't you?"

"Which school?" I inquired.

"The elementary school here in town."

"Oh, you mean the school that speaks, the English Speaking School. Yes. I have four kids in it, as a matter of fact. And there will be one more next September. Her name is . . . "

"Yeah. I thought you had quite a few going there. Which brings up my reason for dropping in to see you today."

"Am I behind in my tuition?" I asked.

"No. It's something else. One of the school board members is leaving Switzerland in a month or so, and I thought that since you're new here and have some children in the school, you might consider serving on the board on an interim basis until the Association meets in June."

"But, I don't know anything about school boards or education. I've only been to one PTA meeting in my life, and I was almost thrown out of that for speaking up against the progressive system. What happens in June?" I inquired.

"Well . . . you will be one of the nominees and, if elected, you can serve a term as a full-fledged board member."

"How many members on the board?"

"Five," he said. "Three Americans, a Britisher, and a Canadian. The chairmanship rotates each year or so according to seniority."

"That doesn't sound too bad," I said. "At least I won't be in charge for a few years. I guess I'll go along with it."

"Fine," he said. "Take it easy."

"You too," I replied.

When he left my office, I flipped through some of my papers for a brochure on the English Speaking School of Bern. I found it, and it read:

> *The English Speaking School of Bern is a private, non-profit day school for boys and girls, ages four to fourteen years, offering curriculum from kindergarten through the equivalent of the American eighth grade. The school was founded in October 1961 for the purpose of providing English-language education for children of English-speaking residents of the Bern area. It is the only institution in Bern offering an English-language curriculum and thus fulfills a vital need for dependents of diplomatic and business personnel. A consistently high attendance since the founding of the school is a testimony to the high standard of instruction provided. There are some sixty children enrolled, representing ten nationalities. The school curriculum is a carefully-weighed balance of . . .*

It's a nice school, I thought. My children were doing well in it and liked their teachers. There was a problem though. It was housed in two small rented apartments and was filled almost to capacity.

It just so happened that by the time the June Association meeting rolled around, all three of the Americans had resigned from the school board. The British and Canadian members remained, but declined to assume the chairmanship. Within the short span of two months, I found myself not only a full-fledged member, but chairman of the board and President of the Association for the Promotion of the English Speaking School of Bern. I have never been able to figure that one out. At any rate, two other American Embassy officers were elected to the board, and the Association adjourned for the summer.

In late August, I received a report from the headmaster that seventy-two pupils were enrolled for the term beginning in

September. "How many children will the apartments hold?" I inquired.

"Well," he said, "the way the classes are set up, we can accommodate sixty-eight in the six rooms, and there will be an overage of four fifth-graders."

"Let's see," I said, "the school started in 1961 with fifty-five students. That's an increase of four or five a year."

"It's worse than that," the headmaster said. "There has been a progressive rise. We have a net increase of ten this year, and it could well go up an additional twenty next year."

"I wonder where they're all coming from," I said. "Never mind. About the overflow; do we have any place to put them?"

"There's a small kitchen," he replied.

"Into the kitchen they go," I said. "We mustn't turn anyone away. Besides, we can't afford it."

I called a meeting of the school board to discuss the very serious problem of the overcrowding situation. A study of the records had revealed that everybody had wanted a new school building, but there had been two problems—finding the money to build one and locating a place to put it. I had the feeling that if we could solve the first problem, the second could hardly be an obstacle. According to the records, there had been a couple of attempts to locate land, but absolutely no indication as to what should be done once a tract of land was found. The accounts of the school showed a total wealth of four thousand dollars. A new building would cost anywhere from fifty to seventy thousand dollars. There were forty families in the school association, and they were transient in nature. To split the cost among them would call for a one-time assessment of one to two thousand dollars per family in addition to the tuition rates. We would price ourselves out of business as a school. It so happened that the Canadian board member had recently received a nibble on a piece of land in Gümligen, a suburb of Bern. "Let's look at the property," I said, adjourning the meeting.

We saw the land, liked it, and made a deal with the owner to give us a six months rent-free option on it while we attempted to raise some money. I went to three banks and asked about the terms for a loan on a new school building costing fifty thousand dollars plus. They all gave the same answer: "You raise one-half, and we'll lend you the rest." I went home, poured myself a bourbon, and drew up a document entitled, "Building Fund Campaign for the English Speaking School of Bern," which began as follows:

> *A fund-raising campaign is hereby inaugurated for the purpose of financing the construction of a new building in Gümligen for the English Speaking School of Bern. Occupancy is envisaged by the beginning of the 1966-67 school year. The target figure for the campaign is two hundred thousand Swiss francs ($46,500 U.S.). The primary area for soliciting contributions will be Switzerland, including, of course, the association membership itself . . .*

I called another board meeting at which I discussed my campaign, pounded on the table, and announced, "We shall have our new building in the fall." It was so convincing, I almost believed it myself.

I approached thirteen influential leaders, including the Mayor of Bern, all of whom agreed to be patrons of the building fund campaign. I then drew up an appeal letter and sent it to 2,600 individuals, companies, and organizations. We qualified as an "American-sponsored" school abroad, so I applied through the Embassy to the Department of State for financial help. The money started rolling in from all over Switzerland. By February 1966, we had received more than ten thousand dollars in voluntary contributions from thirty-five cities and communities. The

Department of State came through with a ten thousand dollar grant.

With the campaign just three months old, we were sure to raise the additional five thousand dollars. I took the good news to the Schweizerische Volksbank in Bern and was overjoyed when the bank gave its approval on a loan. We picked a builder, who broke ground on June 1. In September, when the building was nearly completed, I swiped the old school sign from the apartment and placed it among my foreign service souvenirs. On October 12, 1966, no less than 107 students of fourteen nationalities marched through the new entrance. The official opening ceremony for the building was held on December 3. Among the more than 150 attendees were the Mayor of Bern and six ambassadors. Speeches were delivered and champagne was served. On December 5, I sent a letter to the school board announcing my resignation as of February 1, 1967; this was a little promise I had made to myself.

The development of the English Speaking School is an excellent example of international cooperation in the field of education. The founding of the school was American-inspired, its curriculum American-oriented, and the achievement of the new building was in large measure attributed to the ingenuity and drive of the American board members. However, the participation by other nationals has been an essential feature of the management, operation, and success of the school since its inception, and the school has quite properly maintained its private international character. It was, in fact, the international character of the project that appealed to Switzerland's policy of promoting international solidarity and brought forth voluntary contributions from many individuals and organizations having no direct or even indirect interest in the school.

One of my more pleasant duties as chairman of the school board had been to officiate at graduation ceremonies, and it was my honor in June 1966 to present a diploma to daughter number four, Louise. It was at the same time a sad occasion, because it meant that Louise would have to join the ranks of our away-from-home school children in the fall. With the removal of U.S. forces from France, the high school at Dreux phased out of existence. However, the American High School in Munich began accepting seven-day boarders, so we registered Catherine, Joan, and Louise there. That September Theresa began her second year at college. Although there were now four girls away at school, at least they were together in the same city and within relatively close reach by minibus, eight hours on a clear day. We drove the little ones to Munich several times that school year primarily to get cheeseburgers and milkshakes at the Army snackbar, but also to see the girls.

Jackie was certainly no less busy in Switzerland with her projects than she had been in England. In the fall of 1964, when we had been in the Silvahof Hotel just a little over a month, she became one of five members of a committee established to create an English Language Lending Library to provide leisure reading for—of all things—the English-speaking community. In less than three months, the gals had collected and cataloged two thousand books and found rent-free space in a local church basement. Jackie was the first chairman of the library and was an active participant in the duty roster for almost three years.

During my two-year stint as chairman of the school board, she not only tolerated my raving and ranting about the fund-raising campaign but served as hostess and provided refreshments at the school association meetings. She was also a "room mother" and devoted many hours to working on school parties and driving little kiddies to their weekly ice-skating treat. On one excursion to the ice rink, Jackie loaded the minibus with fourteen children and pulled off. Three minutes later, the headmaster noticed little five-year-old Ellen standing outside the school all alone with her ice skates draped by her side.

"What are you doing here, Ellen?" he asked.

"I'm waiting for my Mommy to take me skating."

"But your Mommy has already left," he said.

"No she hasn't," Ellen replied. A moment later, Jackie had instinctively doubled back to pick up Ellen. "I told you she'd be here," Ellen called back, scrambling into the car.

In her spare time, Jackie also contributed her dish-washing talents to the annual bazaar for the International Protestant Missions. Moreover, she prepared excellent representation dinners and lunches for my diplomatic and business contacts, not to mention teas and coffee sessions for a goodly number of the better-halves around town. She continued to be at my side through the numerous cocktail parties and receptions in Bern. And with all this, neither the house nor the family collapsed. I marveled at her energy and sometimes wondered if the wrong one was drawing the paycheck.

In the spring of 1966, I went out for the Embassy softball team. I did this primarily because the Embassy had lost the year before in its annual game against the U.S. Mission in Geneva, but also because I was overweight and needed the exercise. Largely as a result of my participation, the team lost again. What I mean is that I failed to hit a home run in the last inning when we were behind thirteen to seven.

In the spring of 1967, things were different. Malcolm Jr. was sixteen years old. He had played a little baseball at the Villa St. Jean in Fribourg and volunteered to join me in the Embassy practice sessions leading up to the game with Geneva. We puttered around on Saturday afternoons for a couple of months. Malcolm Jr. was assigned to second base as an alternate, and I became fairly well-entrenched in left field (primarily because I was left-handed). The big game with the Geneva Mustangs was set for Saturday, June 10. Malcolm and I were all fired up to play. Then we heard that Catherine was to graduate from the American High School in Munich on the evening of June 9. We certainly didn't want to miss Cathy's graduation. But what about the game?

Jackie and I took off in the minibus for Munich at ten o'clock in the morning on June 9. We arrived in time for dinner with Catherine and attended the graduation ceremony. We picked up Catherine's luggage, and the three of us departed for Bern at 11:30 P.M. I drove all night and reached Effingerstrasse at 8:30 in the morning. I set the alarm for 10:30 and went to bed to get a little rest before the two-and-a-half-hour drive to Geneva.

The game started promptly at two. I was put in right field, much to my surprise, where the sun beat down into my already bleary eyes. I didn't make one error, largely because no balls were hit to my field. I got one hit but was put out stealing home. Malcolm Jr. was sent into the game at second base in the fifth inning. By the beginning of the top half of the seventh and last inning, the score stood: Geneva Mustangs, ten; Bern Bears, seven. Malcolm started off with a double, the rest of the gang came through, and the Bern Bears won a thrilling squeaker, eleven to ten. Wow!

Chapter Ten

HOME-LEAVE AND RETURN FOR MORE

In mid-1967 it was home-leave time again. Jackie packed everything everybody needed for a ten-day cruise on the SS *Independence,* a six-week stay in America, and a five-day return trip on the SS *United States.* We took the early morning train from Bern to Genoa on July 5 and boarded the ship at five in the afternoon. There were three days of rubber-necking stops on the Mediterranean—Monte Carlo, Cannes, Barcelona, and Alicante. We had, of course, seen the main tourist attractions in Monte Carlo before. So this time we spent the allotted three hours there roaming the streets and window-shopping. At Cannes, while Jackie took the rest of the children swimming in the sea, I spent a pleasant hour and a half in a French dentist's office with Frances and her ailing molar. Barcelona was Barcelona, if you know what I mean. It was market day in Alicante, and we had a ball buying large hats and handbags. Malcolm and Joan almost missed the ship, but pulled up in a taxi just before the gangplank was removed. Except for an exciting twenty-four hour storm one day out of Gibraltar, the trip was great. Guess who played drums on Passenger Entertainment Night?

Home-leave was really something this time. We rented a tremendous cottage at Bay Ridge, Maryland. By tremendous, I mean it held all eleven of us and had room for five or six more. For the third home-leave in a row, my brother-in-law (who ran an automobile agency) arranged to provide us with the snazziest station wagon afloat. The first week home, I drove the wagon to Washington each day for consultations and in the process notified a few of our old friends of our whereabouts. From then on, carload after carload of people, some of whom we knew, visited us "for the day" to partake in swimming (the water was forty feet from our front door), eating, beer drinking, and folksy chatter. Meals for twenty to twenty-five people were not infrequent. I became known as the keeper of the eternal charcoal flame. For five weeks I stood in the yard tending hamburgers and hot dogs. Thank God somebody put a beer in my hand every now and then; otherwise I would have died of thirst.

For the most part, the conversations with our friends were interesting. We discussed the merits of travel, the racial problem, Vietnam, hippies, politics, children, and money. With some people though, we found conversation hard to come by. I recall one situation in particular with a former high school chum. "Well, Malky," he said, "you've been overseas for a long time. What is it? Five years?"

"No," I replied, turning three hamburgers over. "We've been abroad for nine years. We were six years in London and three . . . "

"Like I said, it's a long time. What's it like over there? I mean, what are the people like?"

"Well," I said, "people are basically the same the world over. In Europe, despite the creation of regional groups, there is still strong evidence of nationalism, probably for historical . . ."

"Do they play baseball over there?" he asked.

"No. But they have other games, such as cricket, soccer, and . . ."

"Did you see that crazy fight on TV the other night? Hey! My beer's gone. Where do you keep it?"

"In the kitchen. Bring me one please," I said to his back. I looked up at his bikini-clad wife who was slinking in my direction.

"Honey, you're cooking those damned things too much," she said.

"I can put on a fresh one. Or perhaps you would prefer to eat it raw."

"Nah! Actually, I'm fresh out of bourbon. You fixing 'em out here or where?"

"In the kitchen," I replied. "Your husband is in there. Maybe he can fix you up."

"That's what you think," she said.

"C'est la vie," I commented.

"Oh, you speak Spanish."

"Just a smidgen," I admitted.

She twirled around twice and headed toward the kitchen, deflecting the atmosphere from side to side with her generous hips. I watched with academic interest, comparing her to Jackie. After each of our nine children, Jackie had snapped back like a rubber band to the same weight and figure she had at age twenty. This woman—while not bad—apparently had no such elasticity and, after three children, certainly did not do justice to a bikini. In the meantime, the three hamburgers burned to a crisp. Some heated words flowed out of the kitchen, followed by my friend and his wife. She turned toward the beach with her bourbon to rejoin the others, and he continued in my direction with two cans of beer. I tossed the burned burgers into the garbage pail, and we sat down on a picnic bench to quench our thirst.

"That woman!" he said. "I can never satisfy her."

"I know . . . uh, I mean, what's the matter?" I asked.

"Oh, she always wants to go somewhere. We were having a fight in the kitchen about our vacation this summer. She wants to go to Ocean City, Maryland."

"What's wrong with that?" I asked. "It would be a change of scenery."

"I'm not going to drive her two hundred miles just so she can parade around in her bikini. We have a nice backyard. I don't see why she can't be contented to stay home and enjoy it. I like to relax and watch a good ball game on TV, but she can't see it my way."

"Where did you go last summer?"

"Nowhere," he said. "And that's her gripe. I keep telling her that people travel because they think the grass is always greener someplace else, and, of course, it isn't."

"A little variety wouldn't hurt," I commented.

"Sure. It's different with you," he said. "You have to travel; that's your job. But I bet deep down, you and Jackie feel you've missed the security of a real home base, especially when you have to put up with a lot of foreigners."

"I suppose you're right," I said. "We have had to suffer the drudgery of crossing the Atlantic several times on luxury liners, eating three large meals a day. In addition to my day-to-day duties at the embassies in London and Bern, I have had to spend weeks attending conferences in such God-forsaken places as Vienna, Paris, Frankfurt, Berlin, Cardiff, Hamburg, and twice in Dublin. I even had to go back to London this spring to attend a course in international political relations. Jackie has had the misfortune of going to most of these places with me. Moreover, we have had to resort to taking our vacations on the French Riviera, in the Swiss Alps, and on Lake Maggiore in northern Italy. We had to get all dressed up and go to Buckingham Palace—not once but twice. It was part of our official duties to be dragged into two diplomatic outings in Switzerland. The more difficult one was when we took a special train to the Lake of Thun and embarked on two luxury cruisers which had been tied together for the occasion. Those stupid ships toured the lake for two hours at the foot of the Alps, while four hundred diplomats and a whole host of Swiss government officials were obliged to drink champagne, talk, and munch on assorted hors d'oeuvres. After that, we were forced into an old castle—at Oberhofen—and there had to listen to Swiss Alpine horns and watch folk dances as we consumed a meal the likes of which we had never known. It has also been my sad luck to attend scores of intimate dinners and business luncheons, exchanging boring ideas with prominent government types and successful businessman. Jackie and I have been roped into serving as planning and escort team for governors, congressmen, and other VIPs, putting up with more meals, tours, and receptions free of charge. Because we had children in a small private school in Switzerland, I was shanghaied into becoming chairman of the board, and then when a new school building was constructed during my term, I had to suffer the embarrassment of a lot of local publicity—I became incensed at the sight of my picture in the papers. Perhaps the most agonizing thing has been driving all over Europe for nine years with CD on my bumper, a symbol which gave me diplomatic immunity even when I wanted to be arrested. Man, it's rough."

"Are you trying to pull my leg or something?" he asked.

"No," I replied, throwing my empty beer can across the lawn. I jumped up and announced, "Last one in the water is narrow-minded." He made it before I did, incidentally.

On August 24, we packed everything and everybody except our oldest daughter and took the night train to New York. Theresa stayed behind to start her third year at the University of Maryland in College Park. The SS *United States* headed toward Le Havre the next day. With the great variety of food served on board, we were quickly persuaded off of our hamburger diet. Not a ripple on the water all the way.

We took the morning boat-train from Le Havre to Paris, arriving at St. Lazare station around noon. While our baggage was being cleared, I asked a porter to hail three or four taxis to take us to Gare de l'est. He told me he had a friend with a limousine who could take us to the other rail station for half the price of four taxis. "But there are ten of us," I said, "and we have seventeen pieces of luggage, including three heavy footlockers." The porter consulted with his friend, a six-foot two-inch, 350-pound Tunisian, who guaranteed that he could do the job in one trip. We all marched out to his limousine, a 1947 black Cadillac. "We'll never make it in that," I said. He put fourteen pieces of luggage on the roof rack and three in the front seat. Ann and Ellen were placed on the cases in front, and the remaining eight started climbing into the back. I was the last one in and could have sworn that big old buggy was crying "Help."

Three blocks outside of the station, the car started smoking. In the middle of what appeared to be the busiest intersection in the world, the brakes locked, and the car wouldn't budge an inch. Crowds gathered to see this strange sight, horns started honking, and French words I had never heard began flowing in our direction. That crazy car loaded down with luggage and eleven people was just sitting there smoking. We began hailing taxis and unloading the limousine. The spectators got quite a show without paying admission. It took four taxis after all. I rode back in the third one to "settle" with my Tunisian friend. His original asking price had been seventy francs. I asked him, in view of the circumstances, what a fair settlement would be. He said the luggage was heavier than he had thought and asked me for one hundred francs. I told him that was very reasonable from his point of view for having taken us three blocks. I gave him twenty-five francs for his effort and departed in the fourth taxi. I had the feeling I could have bought the car for seventy-five.

Our train from Gare de l'est was late arriving in Basel. It pulled in at 10:10 P.M., and the last train to Bern was scheduled to depart at 10:13. We ran down the platform to the customs office, explained that we had a train to catch, flashed our passports, indicated that our baggage was being forwarded through to Bern, and swore that we had nothing with us to declare. I heard the warning whistle for the Bern train. "Let's go kids," I said.

"You can't make that train," the customs man yelled. We joined hands and ran down the steps, across the concourse, and up the opposite steps to our platform. The train started edging out, and we raced down the platform after it. Our big kids grabbed the little ones and pulled them aboard. Men in uniform were feverishly blowing their whistles. The train increased its speed. Jackie got on. Malcolm was charging ahead of me. "Get on, Pop," he said. "No. You first," I screamed. He jumped on. I put on the fastest middle-age gallop I could muster, grabbed a handrail, and swung myself into a car. The family had entered the train through a number of different doors. We assembled after a few minutes, found an empty compartment, and sat down howling our heads off with laughter. The compartment door opened, and the conductor said, "Tickets, please."

"Oh, Malc," Jackie said, "you ought to write a book."

"Maybe I shall," I replied, loosening my tie and checking my wallet to see if I had any Swiss francs to pay the taxis in Bern.

We quickly fell back into the routine. The girls unpacked and repacked for the trip to Munich. Catherine was embarking on her freshman year at the University of Maryland Extension School; Joan was going back for her senior year at high school; Louise was a sophomore. After six years in boys' schools, Malcolm Jr. joined the Munich ranks. We were left with only four children: Joseph, Frances, Ann, and Ellen, all of whom continued on at the English Speaking School.

Jackie resumed her work on a country fair organized by the American Embassy Wives' Group for the benefit of the English Speaking School. The project was initiated and sponsored by the wife of the American Ambassador. The planning had begun early in 1967. The American wives were placed in charge of committees and enlisted the help of many individuals from other elements of the English-speaking and diplomatic circles as well as the local Swiss community. The American Embassy husbands were also "selected" to serve on the committees. After many months of planning and work sessions, the Bern Country Fair 1967 was held on September 30. It was a real piece of Americana in Switzerland, with hot dogs, hamburgers, corn on the cob, bingo, pony rides, children's games, a country store, a spook house, and a grand drawing of more than forty elegant prizes donated by American subsidiary companies located in Switzerland. The girls proved to be no amateurs. When all was said and done, a cool net profit of $5,300 was turned over to the school. Not only that, but everybody had fun. A noble and successful venture indeed. Hats off to the ladies.

In addition to serving on Jackie's bingo committee, I found myself quite busy at the office with two major export promotion events—a trade mission and a trade exhibition. In October, we hosted a fairly large cocktail party at which numerous people in government, business, and diplomatic walks of life asked each other, "How are you?" and heard in reply "I'm fine, thanks; and you?" Except for Theresa, the family was together again in November when we had a twenty-one-pound turkey for

Thanksgiving. They returned from school in December, of course, for Christmas. Ellen was seven years old on January 7, 1968 and received ski pants, a blouse, and a puzzle. For Malcolm's seventeenth birthday early in May, I sent a check to Munich for his use in purchasing some garments suitable for a boy his age plus a desperate request that he have his hair cut with the change. I sealed the letter and, with the end of a black U.S. Government ballpoint pen in my mouth, contemplated the remaining nine birthdays that would descend upon our family during the year. It was at that moment that I put pen to scratch pad, made some rapid calculations, and put forth an amazing, money-saving proposition to Jackie.

"You know, Jacq, since our marriage, we have celebrated a total of 169 birthdays in our little family. At an estimated expenditure of $25 per birthday, there has been an outlay of some $4,225. I hereby propose that we henceforth celebrate everybody's birthday on the same day each year and that we call that day Christmas."

"Oh goody," Jackie retorted. "Then we could all get twice as many presents." Having failed to solve that problem, I switched my efforts to an article I was preparing on how to improve the United States balance of payments situation. Jackie walked over, kissed me on the cheek, and quietly stole upstairs to start another one of her famous packing jobs. Our ten-year period of overseas duty was drawing to a close.

We left Switzerland by jet on July 5, 1968. The furniture followed by surface seven weeks later. We settled down into our new home in Chevy Chase, Maryland and girded ourselves for the impending cultural shock following our decade abroad. But that's another story.

Jackie and I enjoy an evening out at the Talk o' the Town nightclub in London, fall of 1959. But fun turned to fear on the 27-mile trip home to Dorking on a foggy, foggy night.

Our home in Hampstead Garden Suburb, north London, 1961-64, the land of Rolls-Royces, Bentleys, Jaguars, and our 1954 Ford station wagon. Frances helps us show off baby Ellen, January, 1961.

Everybody has a job. The Lawrences boarding the SS *America* for home-leave, July, 1961. Jackie is carrying baby Ellen.

Frances, Ann and Joseph at a children's party on the SS *America*, July, 1961.

Here we are all dressed up in our Hampstead, London living room, fall of 1961. Left to right, top: Malcolm Jr., Joan, Theresa, Jackie, Ellen (in Jackie's lap), me, Catherine, Louise. Bottom: Joseph, Frances, Ann.

The Lord Mayor of Bristol, England, telling me a story, April, 1962.

I am kept busy at the Spring Trade Fair in Dublin, Ireland, 1962.
I had a nice chat with Brendan Behan, the Irish playwright, who visited
our booth later that day.

Jackie and I visit the Queen of England.

3

E II R

The Lord Chamberlain is
commanded by Her Majesty to invite
Mr. Malcolm Lawrence
and Mrs. Lawrence
to an Afternoon Party in the Garden of Buckingham Palace
on Tuesday, the 24th July 1962, from 4 to 6 o'clock p.m.
(Weather Permitting)
Morning Dress or Uniform or Lounge Suit.

Ann, Frances and Joseph with American poet, Jonathan Williams,
U. S. Trade Center, London, November, 1962. This little group appeared
in *The London Times*.

Again at the November 1962 exhibit. Ann watches Santa go up the chimney; or is he coming down? Nine years later, this picture found its way to the front page of the Christmas issue of the *Bethesda-Chevy Chase Tribune* in Montgomery County, Maryland.

The Lawrence family visiting a toy exhibition at the U. S. Trade Center in London, January, 1963. Left to right: Jackie, Theresa, Catherine, Joan, Malcolm Jr., Louise, Joseph, Frances, Ann and Ellen. The kids were thrilled to see their picture in the *Evening Standard* newspaper the next day.

A U.S. DEPARTMENT OF COMMERCE PUBLICATION

International Commerce

April 22, 1963

"*U.S. toys are status symbols*"—A. C. Gilbert

Malcolm Jr. and Joseph were so intrigued by the trains at the U. S. Trade Center toy exhibit in London, January, 1963, that they made the cover of a U. S. Government publication.

Chateau d'Oberhofen on the Lake of Thun, Switzerland, with American
Embassy Counselor and Mrs. Henry Cox and Mrs. Franz Weber,
wife of the Swiss Vice Chancellor, June 25, 1965.

Jackie and I are greeted by American Ambassador and Mrs. True Davis
at their July 4, 1965, garden party, Bern, Switzerland.

The gang at the American Embassy in Bern, Switzerland, in July of 1965, after a 20-year length-of-service ceremony for me. Left to right: Louise, Malcolm Jr., Theresa, Joseph, Catherine, Frances, Ann and Ellen. Top row: the author, Jackie and Joan.

General Motors Suisse Managing Director Nurnberg is saying something amusing about Jackie and me, in Bienne, Switzerland, August, 1965.

From the U. S. Department of State *Newsletter* June 1966: Henry J. Kellermann, Chargé d'Affaires of the American Embassy in Bern, Switzerland, presents a $10,000 U. S. Government education grant to Commercial Attaché Malcolm Lawrence, who is Chairman of the Board of Directors of the English Speaking School of Bern. The grant will be used to finance part of the construction cost of a new school building. Looking on are Jack Smith, left, Economic Officer, and James N. Leaken, Administrative Officer, who are also on the Board of Directors.

The new English Speaking School of Bern in the opening day dawn, October 12, 1966.

U. S. Department of Commerce official Jim Lefever and I watching the crowd at the U. S. Nuclear Exhibition in Basel, Switzerland, September, 1966. The gentleman touching his nose is Hans Schaffner, the President of Switzerland.

Here I am holding hands with President Lyndon Johnson at the Nuclear Exhibition.

Fall of 1966 - this time according to height. Left to right: the author, Jackie, Malcolm Jr., Catherine, Joan, Theresa, Louise, Joseph, Frances, Ann and Ellen. This was taken in our home at 54 Effingerstrasse in the heart of Bern, Switzerland.

On the left, Catherine, Jackie and I watch our horses lose in the lounge of the SS *United States,* returning to Switzerland after home-leave, August, 1967. On the right, Marty Stahl, the Director of the U. S. Trade Center in Milan, and his wife.

Malcolm with American Ambassador John Hayes and Jackie with the wife of Swiss Vice Chancellor Franz Weber at a country fair to raise funds for the English Speaking School, Bern, Switzerland, fall of 1967.

Sitting in with the band at the U. S. Marines Ball, Bern,
Switzerland, 1967.

Political Counselor Herman Skofield (left) and Economic Officer Jack
Smith help me say good-bye to Switzerland, 1968.

The birds return to the nest frequently. Lawrence children,
Thanksgiving, 1980. Top, left to right: Malcolm Jr., Ann, Joseph.
Middle: Joan, Frances, Louise and Ellen. Bottom: Catherine and Theresa.
This is my all-time favorite photo of the "kids."

Jackie and I, both members of the class of 1943, attend the 55th reunion
of Coolidge High School graduates, May 16, 1998.

Chapter Eleven

A SUSTAINING NOTE

Predestination can exist only in a vacuum or among the very rich. For most of us, the walk through life is a series of linked but unpredictable steps, sometimes straight, but usually zig-zag. Man is born with drive, determination, and willpower and must, in a sense, pull himself through life by his own boot straps. However, his efforts are constantly being challenged and affected by outside forces which frequently alter his course and lead him into the all important step toward his ultimate destination.

In my own case, the biggest outside force appeared at age twenty when Jackie presented me with the leather bookbag. On the surface it seems like a trivial thing, but if that event had not taken place, this book might well have been entitled, *Memoirs of a Left-Handed Drummer Who Played Right-Handed.*

But it wasn't and I'm glad. I'm glad I received the bookbag, glad I went to college, glad I married Jackie, glad we had nine children, and glad I joined the Foreign Service. Admittedly, a large family aggravates the logistical problems encountered in a

Foreign Service career, and we found little glamour in filling out forms, taking medical examinations, packing our stuff, closing down houses, traveling with umpteen suitcases and crates, clearing customs, finding new houses, and dealing with education problems. But these hardships were greatly overshadowed by the thrills and rewards reaped from serving the United States abroad, and I thank my lucky stars for the health, happiness, and adventures we have enjoyed.

At this advanced stage of my life, I still believe in God, mankind, my wife, our family unit, the United States of America, the community, education, ambition, common sense, honesty, hard work, clean living, exercise, good food, and myself—though not necessarily in that order. But most of all, I believe that something will come along again and again to make life more interesting and challenging.

At the end of Chapter Ten, I said that in the summer of 1968 we "girded ourselves for the impending cultural shock following our decade abroad." And what a shock it was.

While we were overseas, Jackie and I held on to the principles of what it was to be Americans and remembered the high ideals and standards of American education. But when we returned home to Montgomery County, Maryland, there was a rude awakening. The education of a decade earlier no longer existed. The schools had taken a drastic turn for the worse. And through our investigations, we discovered that the problems were nationwide.

We found that discipline was ragged. Student revolt was becoming a fashionable tool for destroying the schools. School boards were catering to weakness and succumbing to every whim of permissive superintendents and demanding student bodies, and drug abuse was rampant in the schools and growing at a significant rate.

The curriculum and teaching methods had changed drastically. Unevaluated experimental innovations had begun to permeate the schools, crowding out the basics. To keep students "happy," emphasis was shifting from what a child should know to how a child should feel. There was a loss of scholarly objectivity and academic freedom. Chronological factual history was being replaced by conceptualized social studies. Achievement scores were on the decline; the schools were inflating grades, handing out social promotions, and graduating functional illiterates.

We noted the introduction of open-ended, non-judgmental discussions based not on what was right or wrong, but on how students viewed such concepts as lying, cheating, stealing, and expression of human sexuality. Situational ethics were invading the schools big time, with the children being told to consider all options of moral and ethical issues and "make up their own minds" as to what to believe and do. We felt that community ethics and standards were being eroded and that the schools were actually contributing to the delinquency of minors.

State laws and county regulations were being violated. The classroom materials invaded the privacy of the students and the family. Teachers were rolling over and playing dead to the voices of parents and instead were listening to the tunes of the new educationists and curriculum developers who were dishing out instructions to use such psychotherapeutic techniques as role-playing, psycho-drama, and socio-drama. Without parental permission, teachers were assuming the role of clinicians and therapists—and the children were the patients.

Jackie and I were most concerned about the prospects for our children's education. To combat some of these tragic directions, we organized parental groups and flew into action.

Much of the "action" story has been told in my two-volume book entitled *Tilting at Societal Ills and Other Capers from the Lawrence Papers—1969-1998* that was published in November 1998. Excerpts from that book, including the Introduction and

"So Who is Malcolm Lawrence?" are provided as Appendix I to this book.

Copies of *Tilting at Societal Ills* are in a number of prestigious libraries, including those of President George W. Bush, the U.S. Department of State, the Library of Congress (Exchange Division), the George Washington University (Washington, D.C.), the Montgomery County Historical Society (Rockville, Maryland), the Montgomery County Public Library System (Maryland), Superintendent of Schools Reference Library, Montgomery County Public Schools (Rockville, Maryland), Hillsdale College (Michigan), the Eagle Forum Education Center (St. Louis, Missouri), and a condensed version in the Vatican Library (Vatican City).

I sent the condensed version of *Tilting* to Pope John Paul II as part of a three-volume package on September 20, 2001. The other two volumes were *Facing Facts About Education*, a booklet written and illustrated by my daughter Joan Marie Ciampa, and *A Chronology of Education* compiled by Dr. Dennis Cuddy, an author and historian of Raleigh, North Carolina. In a September 29, 2001, letter from the Vatican, Monsignor Pedro López Quintana wrote me to say:

> The Holy Father has asked me to acknowledge the letter and the three books which you sent to him. He appreciates the sentiments which prompted you to share your thoughts with him.
>
> His Holiness will remember your intentions in his prayers. Upon you and your family he cordially invokes the grace and peace of our Lord Jesus Christ.

I sent the package to Pope John Paul because of his position as one of the spiritual and cultural leaders of the world. I felt that the tragic story of American education should be told far and wide and that the Vatican Library was a logical place for such information to be found and used by researchers and intellectual leaders.

As for Jackie, she has worked for decades to preserve high standards in public education. Her U.S. Congressional testimony and other efforts are also carried in *Tilting at Societal Ills.* Jackie was honored as Woman for the 1980s by the *Montgomery County Advertiser* (Maryland). All this is in addition to being a great mother and a tolerant wife to me for fifty-seven years.

In closing this opus, I wish to provide three recent examples of my freelance work. Appendix 2 is a news release entitled, "Ranking the Twentieth Century Presidents," dated December 20, 1999. It was picked up by a number of papers, including the *Washington Times.* In a letter to the editor, a *Potomac Almanac* (Maryland) reader said, "I thought it was an interesting twist debunking the liberal mythology of who the great presidents are. I found it enlightening to say the least." On the other hand, another *Almanac* reader sent me an anonymous letter laced with four-letter words. Make up your own list. It's fun.

Appendix 3 is a December 14, 2000 news release entitled, "Humpty Dumpty's Fall." It deals with the Gore/Bush presidential election, one of the most phenomenal events in our political history. *The Montgomery Journal,* the daily paper of Montgomery County, Maryland, carried the release under the headline, "For Candidate Gore, the Votes Simply Weren't There."

Finally, I provide in Appendix 4 a nostalgic piece entitled, "Fran Grady and the D.C. Swing Era." I wrote this in April 2002 at the request of Lucille Grady, Fran Grady's widow. Fran was in my view the best tenor saxophone player in town during the swing era. The article was sent to many former Washington musicians, reproduced by them and mailed out to old-timers throughout the country. Comments from a number of big band buffs were gratifying. Also, William Schulz, *Reader's Digest's* editor-at-large in Washington, wrote, "I found it fascinating, although a decade and a half or so before my time." *Washington Post* senior editor John Cotter called the article "a treasure trove of names and places that I fear will soon slip away from us." Maybe it won't slip away altogether; the Fran Grady article is made available to researchers by The Historical Society of Washington, D.C.

I cannot think of any better way to end this book than to say GOD BLESS MY FAMILY and GOD BLESS AMERICA.

EXCERPTS FROM *TILTING AT SOCIETAL ILLS AND OTHER CAPERS FROM THE LAWRENCE PAPERS— 1969-1998*

Introduction

The items included in *Tilting at Societal Ills* pertain to thirty years of my having a go at some of the major problems facing our country at the national, state and local levels. It is my contention that the two most tragic societal ills are poor quality public education and the abuse of illegal drugs.

In large measure the lingering drug problem since the mid-1960s can be attributed to failure of the public schools to do a proper job of educating our youth. Curriculum and textbooks have been dumbed down, and discipline is in a shambles. The students consequently have become a bored lot, have taken to drugs and more lately are shooting each other on school grounds.

In the midst of the use and exchange of illegal drugs on and around school property, the school authorities have literally looked the other way for decades. The drug curriculum has been a disaster, as the voices of dripping compassion from the mental health approach to drug abuse have driven the hardliners out of the school systems throughout the country. Drugs continue to pour across our borders to meet the domestic demand despite the valiant efforts of our enforcement authorities to cut off supplies.

The decline in education standards is the result of a shift in emphasis from cognitive to affective education—that is from what students know to what students feel. The basics have largely been replaced by techniques and curriculum promoting self-esteem, political correctness, conceptualized social studies, revisionist history and psycho-babble. The use of phonics has virtually been abandoned in favor of the ineffective whole word or so-called look-say method of reading instruction.

It doesn't matter these days what students learn. It's a question of how they feel about themselves. Former U.S. Senator Samuel I. Hayakawa said it best when he warned the Senate in 1978: "An educational heresy has flourished, a heresy that rejects the idea of education as the acquisition of knowledge and skills ... the heresy of which I speak regards the fundamental task in education as therapy." In point of fact, the students don't really feel good about themselves, and "there's the rub." In fact, it's a double rub: the students are not happy, and they are not experiencing good education discipline.

Not only are the products of our public schools running well behind the standards of many other countries, but our high school graduates are rarely able to compute, express themselves orally or put a decent series of written sentences together. As a result, students at the college freshman level throughout the United States are forced to attend remedial courses in reading, writing and math before attending the regular classes.

Career prospects for our youth and the status of our national economy are made even worse by the steady decline in the quality of education in our colleges and universities. Take a look at some of the weird courses being offered today. Things are so bad that corporations are giving remedial training to college graduates.

Since the passage of the Elementary and Secondary Education Act of 1965, the deterioration in our public schools has been aided and abetted by a growing flow of federal funds to state and local systems to develop a whole host of non-academic nonsense. Education administrators, curriculum developers and poorly trained teachers have gobbled up the monies and refused to bite the hands that feed them. The national and local PTA leadership has joined forces with the school administrators and rubber-stamped the programs of the permissive innovators. The PTA should go back to bake sales and quit trying to please the educators at budget hearings.

The education establishment does not, of course, want its funds diminished in the least, regardless of the poor quality of its output. And so, parents who complain or try to improve educa-tion are seen as disrupters of the money flow and are usually labeled radicals, censors, or budget-cutters. They are derided at school board meetings and chuckled at by the members of the local press, who want to stay in the good graces of the school establishment.

I would love to have a penny for every parent in the United States who has been told by a teacher, "You are the only one to complain." The educators have received guidance from the National Education Association (NEA) on how to deal with com-plaining parents. I believe that the NEA's policies and programs over the years have made a major contribution to the downward slope of the American public education system.

Matters were made worse by the creation of the U.S. Department of Education in 1979, with a budget that increases by billions of dollars each year. That agency was a political reward for the educators who supported the election of Jimmy Carter in

1976. Subsequent Republican administrations did not have the political guts to even try to close it down, despite the fact that Reagan made a campaign promise to do it.

If you try to change the bad habits of educators or put a dent in the flow of drugs, it is in many respects like banging your head against a wall. But the problem is, it doesn't feel better when you stop. Nevertheless, some parents and civic leaders throughout the country still keep trying to improve our society in what seems to be a perpetual uphill battle to save a nation in which moral values and standards are steadily going downhill.

Some specific education-related problems I have dabbled in include the drug abuse policy issue, smoking privileges on school grounds, psychological manipulation of students, invasion of student and family privacy, violations of state by-laws for classroom instruction, the trampling on parental rights, and the dangling of contraceptives and other forms of sex education that have brought about a sexual revolution among America's children in the face of a tragic epidemic of AIDS and other venereal diseases. Incidentally, according to the Centers for Disease Control, Maryland's syphilis rate in 1997 was five times the national average.

The endeavors of parents in the state of Maryland who want to cut wasteful public expenditures and right the wrongs of bureaucracy have been largely ignored by a traditionally liberal Democrat-dominated legislature. And Montgomery County, Maryland, my legal residence for the past forty-eight years, has for decades been oozing with tax-and-spend liberal Democrats who equate liberalism with progress and conservatism with destruction. Montgomery County, which is loaded with lawyers, lobbyists, politicians and highly-paid U.S. government and business executives, is one of the richest areas in the United States. Rather than fight city hall, many of these people simply send their children to private schools and continue to vote for liberals to stay in the social swim. The same thing happens in neighboring Washington, D.C., only worse.

But the problems extend well beyond the state of Maryland and our nation's capital. For evidence of this, one has only to look back to the hearings held in March 1984 by the U.S. Department of Education. Scores of parents throughout the country traveled to seven cities to spell out their accounts of the psychological abuse of children in the public schools. There were thirteen hundred pages of testimony describing how classroom courses have confused school children about life, standards of behavior, moral choices, religious loyalties and relationships with parents and peers. Did the Department of Education publish its hearings? No indeed. That job was courageously undertaken by Phyllis Schlafly, who published more than four hundred pages of excerpts in a book entitled, *Child Abuse in the Classroom* (Pere Marquette Press, Alton, Illinois 62002).

I like to think that not everything with which I have been involved has been in vain. The Montgomery County system did approve a better-than-nothing drug procedure in the 1970s and after much pressure and more than eighteen years finally outlawed smoking on school grounds in December 1987. Also with much reluctance, the school authorities adopted a student privacy policy which was published for all to see in the official Student Rights and Responsibilities document in August 1990. The privacy policy was a major victory shared by both the Parents Who Care group and the Maryland Coalition of Concerned Parents, two organizations that I headed.

In the Parents Who Care legal action against objectionable materials and practices in Montgomery County classrooms, which ran for some five years (1972–1977), we batted five out of twelve on our recommendations and within a short period of time saw the school authorities quietly remove all of the materials to which we had objected.

At the national level, as coordinator of the Maryland Coalition of Concerned Parents, I enjoyed my role campaigning for the protection of children from federally funded programs designed for psychological and psychiatric examination, testing and treatment in the classrooms of America. On September 6, 1984, the U.S. Department of Education published the final version of regulations for the 1978 Protection of Pupil Rights or so-called Hatch Amendment to the General Education Provisions Act.

In its December 3, 1984 newsletter, the National Education Association told its members that the Hatch Amendment "covers every classroom teacher, every teaching method, and all classroom materials." It got the teachers excited. And when my sample parental permission letter went into national distribution,* the NEA and thirty-two other education organizations—the HAC Group—undertook a major campaign to discredit the letter and the Hatch Amendment regulations.

On the drug front, I was involved at the local, state, national and international levels. This is one societal ill that will be around for a long time unless the schools and other segments of society really start cracking down. I like to think that my efforts helped hold the line against the decriminalization of marijuana and other drugs, and that my work in the community and with the U.S. State Department's Office of International Narcotics Control led to a greater understanding of the need for cooperation by each community in every nation in the world. Schools represent the most important focal point in alleviating this problem, and that is why I concentrated so much of my community efforts in that direction.

I selected 665 items from my files. The material is chronological. Reproductions of the selections are as I prepared them for

---

* See News Release following this Introduction.

news releases, testimony, speeches, letters and articles, or as they were picked up by the press. Press items are reproduced as actually shown in the newspapers, magazines, books, and other publications.

I wish to thank my wife Jacqueline for her level-headed advice and participation in all of my causes and endeavors. Jacqueline has given many great talks on education. A report on one of them, as carried in the *Oxon Hill Times* for March 6, 1975, was entered into the Congressional Record on April 8, 1975, by U.S. Senator Strom Thurmond. Her extensive testimony before the U.S. Senate Subcommittee on Education, Arts and Humanities was presented on June 7, 1984.

My daughter Joan Marie Ciampa has demonstrated much courage in her own right in dealing with education problems. Her illustrated book *Facing Facts about Education* is the subject of one of my reviews.

I thank the members and supporters of the organizations for which I served either as leader or spokesman, namely the Montgomery County War on Narcotics League, the Parents Who Care group, the Maryland Coalition of Concerned Parents, Accuracy in Academia, and the Contact America Radio Network. Thanks also to the former owners, editors and staffs of two Montgomery County papers no longer in existence: the *Bethesda-Chevy Chase Tribune* and the *Advertiser*. Through their cooperation, many of my views and activities were brought to light. They share in any victories achieved.

Finally, I have been proud and appreciative of the fact that some of my statements and testimony were entered over the years into the Congressional Record and U.S. Congressional committee hearing prints by Senator Joseph Tydings, Senator Sam Ervin, Senator Jesse Helms, Representative Robert Huber, Representative George Miller and Representative Charles Rangel.

If the collection of *Lawrence Papers* can give courage to other parents and future civic activists and obviate any attempts to reinvent the wheel, then this book will have been a gratifying project indeed.

To such activists, one thing is certain: you need publicity. If you are concerned about an issue and say or write something you believe is profound and no one in the outside world hears it or prints it, you're not doing a whole lot for the cause. I know people who expound on their views in their own living rooms until they are blue in the face, but never express themselves elsewhere or put pen to paper. They tell you what they would do if they were senator, governor, or whatever. But that's no good. Don't be a member of the silent majority. When you get involved in an issue, get the press involved, too. It can pay off.

God bless America. It needs all the help it can get.

Malcolm Lawrence
November 1998
Chevy Chase, Maryland

NEWS RELEASE

Maryland Coalition of Concerned Parents on Privacy Rights in Public Schools
Malcolm Lawrence, Coordinator
January 4, 1985

Parents Urged to Protect Education Rights

The Maryland Coalition of Concerned Parents has launched a nationwide appeal to parents, urging them to preserve their education rights under the law through a letter to their local school board president. On January 4, the Coalition began disseminating a recommended text to serve as the basis for such a letter (attached).

The letter points out that under U.S. law based on legislation and court decisions, parents have the primary responsibility for their children's education, and pupils have certain rights which the schools may not deny. It identifies thirty-four categories of controversial classroom practices and materials currently in use throughout the country, ranging from psychological and psychiatric testing and treatment to one-world government or globalism curriculum, personal journals, and life/death decision games. The letter calls for prior informed and written parental consent before such practices and materials can be used with children.

The recommended letter also indicates that many of the controversial items cited are federally funded and are, therefore, subject to the newly-approved regulations for the Protection of Pupil Rights or so-called Hatch Amendment. The Hatch regulations call for prior parental consent, and violations could result in the withdrawal of federal funds from a school system or other contractor determined by the U.S. Department of Education to be in violation of the law.

In releasing the letter, Coalition Coordinator Malcolm Lawrence stated:

> *Parents throughout the United States are protesting against the curricula content and teaching methods in our public schools. Their complaints range from objectionable propaganda in textbooks, to invasion of privacy in the classroom, to disagreement with the changing trends in educational philosophy, which are threatening the role of the family unit and bringing about a resocialization process for their children. Evidence of displeasure with our schools abounded in the 1984 hearings held in seven cities by the U.S. Department of Education on regulations for the Hatch Amendment.*
>
> *The time has come for parents throughout our country to insist on their rights, and we in the Maryland Coalition urge them to write their local school board president, who is in the best position to establish policy. We hope our draft letter will provide parents with useful guidance.*

The Maryland Coalition of Concerned Parents was formed in 1974 to combat psychological probings, non-academic testing, and invasions of privacy of students and their families by public schools. The Coalition was a strong supporter of the Hatch Amendment, which became law on November 2, 1978, and of its implementing regulations, which became effective on November 12, 1984. Malcolm Lawrence, who was the Coalition's founding coordinator, serves as one of the five parents' representatives designated by the U.S. Department of Education for negotiations with the education establishment on the Hatch Amendment regulations.

Attachment: Recommended text of letter from parent to local school board president.

For further information, contact
Malcolm Lawrence, Coordinator
Maryland Coalition of Concerned Parents

Dear _____,

    I am the parent of _____ who attends/attend _____.

    Under U.S. Law based on well-recognized legislation and court decisions, parents have the primary responsibility for their children's education, and pupils have certain rights which the schools may not deny. Parents have the right to assure that their children's beliefs and moral values are not undermined by the schools. Pupils have the right to have and to hold their values and moral standards without direct or indirect manipulation by the schools through curriculum, textbooks, audio-visual materials, or supplementary assignments.

    Accordingly, I hereby request that my child/children be involved in no school activities listed below unless I have first been given the opportunity to review all of the materials to be used and have given my written approval for their use:

- Psychological and psychiatric examinations, tests, or surveys that are designed to elicit information about attitudes, habits, traits, opinions, beliefs, or feelings of an individual or group;

- Psychological and psychiatric treatment that is designed to affect behavioral, emotional, or attitudinal characteristics of an individual or group;
- Values clarification, including use of moral dilemmas, discussion of religious or moral standards, role playing of situations involving moral issues, open-ended discussions of moral issues, and survival games including life/death decision exercises;
- Education pertaining to alcohol and drug abuse;
- Death education, including abortion, euthanasia, suicide, and use of violence;
- Instruction in nuclear war, nuclear policy, and nuclear classroom games;
- Anti-nationalistic, one-world government or globalism curriculum;
- Education in interpersonal relationships, including family life, discussions of attitudes toward parents, and parenting;
- Education in human sexuality, including premarital sex, extramarital sex, contraception, abortion, homosexuality, group sex and marriages, prostitution, incest, masturbation, bestiality, divorce, population control, and roles of males and females;
- Pornography and any materials containing profanity and/or sexual explicitness;
- Guided fantasy techniques;
- Hypnotic techniques;
- Imagery and suggestology;
- Witchcraft and the occult, including horoscopes and zodiac signs;
- Organic evolution, including the idea that man has developed from previous or lower types of living things;

- Political affiliations and beliefs of student and family;
- Personal religious beliefs and practices;
- Mental and psychological problems potentially embarrassing to the student or family;
- Sex behavior and attitudes of student or family;
- Illegal, anti-social, self-incriminating and demeaning behavior;
- Critical appraisals of other individuals with whom the student has close family relationships;
- Legally recognized privileged and analogous relationships, such as those of lawyers, physicians and ministers.
- Income, including the student's role in family activities and finances;
- Non-academic personality tests;
- Questionnaires on personal life, views, and family;
- Log books, diaries, personal journals and autobiography assignments;
- Sociograms;
- Contrived incidents for self-revelation;
- Sensitivity training, including group encounter sessions, group contact sessions, talk-ins, magic circle techniques, self-evaluation and auto-criticism;
- Strategies specifically designed for self-disclosure, e.g., the zig-zag technique;
- Blindfold walks;
- Isolation techniques;
- Psychodrama;
- Sociodrama.

Many of the classroom practices and materials listed above are federally funded, in whole or in part, and are in use in schools throughout the United States. Such federally-funded activities are subject to newly-issued regulations for the Protection of Pupil Rights or so-called Hatch Amendment to the General Education Provisions Act, which became effective on November 12, 1984.

Under that law, no student shall be required as part of any program administered by the U.S. Department of Education to submit without prior written parental consent to psychiatric or psychological examinations, testing or treatment in which the primary purpose is to reveal information in specified sensitive areas. Full details of the new regulations are contained in the *Federal Register* for September 6, 1984.

These new federal regulations provide a procedure for the filing and reviewing of complaints. Alleged violations should first be filed by parents at the local and state levels. If the matter is not satisfactorily resolved there, then the complaint should be filed with the Family Educational Rights and Privacy Office, U.S. Department of Education, 400 Maryland Avenue S.W., Washington, D.C. 20202. At the federal level, provisions are made first for a voluntary remedy. If that fails, federal funds will be withdrawn from a school system or other contractor determined to be in violation of the law.

The purpose of this letter is to preserve my parental responsibilities and my child's/children's rights under United States law based on legislation and court decisions. I respectfully ask you to provide me with a substantive response to this letter, notify the relevant teachers of my request for review and written permission procedures, and arrange to have a copy of this letter placed and kept in my child's/children's permanent file.

Thank you for your cooperation.

Sincerely,

_____

Commentary by Lawrence

The sample letter was distributed to parents throughout the United States by way of a network of community education groups. The News Release was picked up by both AP and UPI wire services and reported on by major newspapers and education journals nationwide. The letter was reproduced as an appendix in the book *Child Abuse in the Classroom,* edited by Phyllis Schlafly. I appeared on numerous network TV shows and radio programs and taped a program with Voice of America for dissemination overseas. The National Education Association and other groups in the education lobby frantically alerted their memberships by circulating some two million copies of the parental rights letter. Parents nationwide began using the letter with varying degrees of success, but the main value of the massive publicity was that parents and taxpayers throughout the United States were made aware of the harmful and controversial practices and materials in the nation's classrooms.

So Who is Malcolm Lawrence?

Malcolm Lawrence was born in 1925 in Washington, D.C., and has been a legal resident of Montgomery County, Maryland, since 1950.

An Air Force veteran of World War II, Mr. Lawrence was in aerial combat action in Europe.

He holds a bachelor of arts degree with a double major in Foreign Affairs and Economics and a master of arts degree in Government and Economic Policy, both from the George Washington University in Washington.

A career U.S. Foreign Service Officer with the diplomatic rank of First Secretary, Malcolm Lawrence retired in 1978 after more than three decades of government service. In 1979 he was reappointed as a consultant to the Department of State.

Positions with the State Department included:

1950–58   Economic Intelligence Research Specialist, Washington; wrote in-depth reports on manufacturing and construction industries, monetary policy, and banking institutions of Western European countries.

1958–64   Economic Officer, American Embassy, London, England; worked on U.S. trade policy, served as Trade Promotion Officer for first U.S. Trade Center abroad, authored numerous economic and marketing reports.

1964–68   Commercial Attaché, American Embassy, Bern, Switzerland; responsible for U.S. trade policy and promotion in Switzerland, coordinated trade exhibitions and trade missions, authored marketing analysis reports and articles for government publications, and served as principal speechwriter on commercial policy and practices.

1968–70   Trade Promotion Specialist, on loan to the U.S. Department of Commerce; ran conferences and gave promotion talks throughout the United States for the establishment of joint government/industry export associations.

1970–71   International Economics Adviser, State Department Bureau of Economic Affairs; served as adviser to Deputy Assistant Secretary of State on U.S. trade and commercial policy.

1971–77   Special Assistant for International Narcotics Control matters on the staff of the Secretary of State; principal speechwriter for U.S. International Narcotics Control program and policies, prepared information and policy papers, Congressional presentation statements and reports, drafted guidelines for U.S. narcotics control officers stationed abroad. Recipient of White House commendations for work with the President's Cabinet Committee on International Narcotics Control and for serving as chairman of the International Work Group for the 1975 White Paper on Drug Abuse prepared by the White House Domestic Council Drug Abuse Task Force.

1977–78   Member of Caribbean Task Force established to study and recommend ways to increase U.S./Caribbean cooperation in trade and economic development.

1979–85   Reappointed by U.S. Department of State as international relations consultant in the Bureau of Administration's Freedom of Information Program.

On civic efforts, while in Switzerland, Malcolm Lawrence served as chairman of the board of the English Speaking School of Bern, an American-sponsored private school attended by children of seventeen nationalities. During his term of office, he spearheaded a successful fund-raising campaign that resulted in the construction of a new building.

In 1968, after his return to the United States, Mr. Lawrence helped launch a concerted approach to curtail drug abuse in Montgomery County, Maryland; he was a founding member and served as chairman of the War On Narcotics League until 1971. For such efforts, he received the 1971 Community Service Award from the Bethesda-Chevy Chase Chamber of Commerce and the 1971 Citizenship Award from the *Bethesda-Chevy Chase Tribune.*

From 1972 to 1977, Malcolm Lawrence headed a group called Parents Who Care that took the Montgomery County school system to court and through five years of administrative proceedings in a landmark case relating to violations of Maryland State bylaws and invasions of student privacy.

Since 1974, Mr. Lawrence has been coordinator of the Maryland Coalition of Concerned Parents, a network of parents and groups throughout the United States and abroad working to protect privacy rights and improve the quality of education.

In 1985, he served as the first president of Accuracy in Academia, a Washington-based organization established to promote truth and balance in American colleges and universities.

From 1984 to 1987, Mr. Lawrence was Education Consultant for, and weekly commentator on, the Contact America Radio Network, a program emanating from Capitol Hill and broadcasting to more than fifty stations throughout the United States.

He has testified at Congressional and federal executive hearings as well as before Maryland legislative committees and Maryland State and Montgomery County boards of education. His testimony and other statements and articles have been placed in The Congressional Record and in official committee prints.

Mr. Lawrence has been guest speaker, lecturer, and panelist at numerous civic, political and professional meetings and conferences throughout the United States.

In addition to a weekly column in the former *Bethesda-Chevy Chase Tribune,* Malcolm Lawrence has written feature articles appearing in *The Washington Post* and other Washington area papers as well as in such national publications as *Vital Speeches of the Day, Social Education, The National Educator, Education Reporter, The Washington Inquirer, and Human Events.* Lawrence has appeared as a guest on such national TV programs as "The Today Show," "20/20," "The 700 Club," "LateNight America" and "The MacNeil/Lehrer NewsHour," as well as on the Cable News Network. He has also been featured on numerous local, regional, and national radio programs and is listed in *Who's Who in Government.*

Lawrence has had a lifelong interest in music. In 1941 at age fifteen he became a professional drummer in the era of the big bands. A member of the D.C. Federation of Musicians until 1958, Lawrence played college, hotel, and nightclub dates with such leading Washington area dance orchestras as Wally Hughes, Jack Morton, and Lee Maxfield.

Mr. and Mrs. Lawrence reside in Chevy Chase, Maryland.

RANKING THE TWENTIETH CENTURY PRESIDENTS

December 20, 1999
Release from the desk of Malcolm Lawrence

1. Ronald Wilson Reagan (1981–89)—Ended the Cold War and saved the West.

2. Theodore Roosevelt (1901–09)—A trustbuster and conservationist.

3. Harry S. Truman (1945–53)—A tough and honest guy; defied the Soviets.

4. Calvin Coolidge (1923–29)—A government hands-off administrator, what a president should be.

5. Dwight David Eisenhower (1953–61)—Good times and a good president, a better general.

6. George Herbert Walker Bush (1989–93)—A preserver of the Reagan Doctrine, but done in by the economy.

7. William McKinley (1897–1901)—Protector of U.S. interests and sound conservative.

8. William Howard Taft (1909–13)—A TR protegé, good for the country.

9. Woodrow Wilson (1913–21)—Idealist, done in by his League of Nations dream.

10. Richard Milhous Nixon (1969–74)—Left holding the Vietnam bag; good on China, done in by his ego.

11. Franklin Delano Roosevelt (1933–45)—A media puff whose legacy was saved by World War II, but who helped give away half of Europe.

12. Warren Gamaliel Harding (1921–23)—A good man, but a poor judge of subordinates.

13. Herbert Clark Hoover (1929–33)—A brilliant engineer in office at the wrong time.

14. Gerald Rudolph Ford (1974–77)—Pardoned Nixon in an otherwise lackluster term.

15. John Fitzgerald Kennedy (1961–63)—A daddy-made dandy, in way over his head.

16. James Earl Carter (1977–81)—Sulked a lot and gave up the Panama Canal.

17. William Jefferson Clinton (1993–)—An absolute phony known primarily for double-talk and sexcapades.

18. Lyndon Baines Johnson (1963–69)—A boorish and unprincipled leader; created an out-of-control welfare state and engineered the crumbling of American pursuit of victory in Vietnam.

★ *Appendix Three* ★

HUMPTY DUMPTY'S FALL

December 14, 2000
Release from the desk of Malcolm Lawrence

How gratifying it was for me—a Republican residing in Democrat-dominated Montgomery County, Maryland—to surf the TV channels during the five weeks following the November 7 election and watch all the spin and legal maneuvers of the Al Gore team as they attempted without success to swipe the election from George Bush.

The part I enjoyed most was witnessing the sad faces of those liberal talking heads—such as Chris Matthews, Andrea Mitchel, Jim Warren, Mario Cuomo, Lanny Davis, Katrina Vanden Heuvel, Jesse Jackson, and Florida Congressman Bob Wexler after the December 12 U.S. Supreme Court decision. Chris Matthews, for example, appeared to have almost recovered from a crying spell as he frantically explored with his guests Cuomo's last-ditch scheme for Gore to pirate electors from the Bush side prior to conceding. It was nice to see the liberal media finally stew in their own juices.

Lawyers on both sides did an excellent job. It just so happened that Bush won the election and had the law on his side.

And so Gore's lawyers just couldn't put Humpty Dumpty together again.

Despite the civil tone of the concession and acceptance speeches on December 13, over the coming months and years many Democrats will continue to trash George Bush and the U.S. Supreme Court. They just won't accept the fact that they lost the 2000 election. If they remain sore losers, I can't see how they will command much respect in 2002 or 2004.

Let us all remember one thing: it wasn't George W. Bush who forced a decision out of the U.S. Supreme Court. It was Albert Gore Jr. in his futile search for votes that simply were not there. Bush isn't the one who is toast. Let's give him a chance to lead the country.

★ *Appendix Four* ★

FRAN GRADY AND THE D. C. SWING ERA

April, 2002
Release from the desk of Malcolm Lawrence

"He was like God," proclaimed fellow musician Carmen Campagnoli.

For forty years Washington area dancers were treated to the solos and section work of an outstanding saxophone player. His name was Francis J. Grady. He passed away on May 29, 2001, at the age of eighty-six.

Francis, known to everyone as Fran, was revered by many musicians and fans for his performances during the era of swing and big bands. I provide herewith a tribute to Fran, but first offer some words about the Washington music scene during the 1930s and 1940s.

The nation's capital was not a producer of name bands à la New Orleans, Kansas City, Chicago, or New York City. Washington was the birthplace and early stomping grounds of the legendary Duke Ellington, but for the most part, D.C. band leaders and their musicians stuck to home and provided entertainment for the many swing enthusiasts in this government town.

There were, of course, some exceptions that were picked up by name bands and moved out to the national scene, such as drummer Don Lamond (by Sonny Dunham), trumpeter Marky Markowitz (by Charlie Spivak) and trombonist brothers Earl and Rob Swope (by Sonny Dunham and Buddy Rich, respectively). And when big band leaders drifted into Washington to play theater or arena dates, they occasionally employed local musicians to fill in.

Dating from the mid-1930s, some of the local luminaries were Barnee Breeskin, the resident band leader at the Shoreham Hotel Blue Room and composer of the music to "Hail to the Redskins" (Corinne Griffith wrote the words); Sam Jack Kaufman, who led the pit orchestra at the Fox Theater (renamed The Capital); Paul Kain, maestro at the Wardman Park Hotel and the Glen Echo Spanish Ballroom; Bill Downer, leader of the top-notch big band at Club Nightingale in nearby Virginia; and Ralph Hawkins, local leader and sometime drummer with Georgie Auld and Harry James.

Other leaders and bookers around town as I recall were Bill Strickland, Meyer Davis, Jack Morton, Tiny Meeker, Jimmy Gandley, Ray King, Wally Hughes, Washie Bratcher, Sidney Seidenman, Jack Corry, The Trojans, Sammy Ferro, Al Massie, Jack Maggio, Frankie Mann, Don Buckley, Gene Donati, Addie Lawyer, Howard Devron and Lee Maxfield.

The principal hotels for sponsored dances were the Washington, Shoreham, Wardman Park, Mayflower, Roger Smith, Hay-Adams, Hamilton, Statler, Roosevelt, Hotel 2400, the Willard, Cairo, Raleigh, Carlton and the uptown Kennedy-Warren.

Area clubs and music spots included the Madrillon, Lotus, Casino Royal, Kavakos, Brinkley's, Louisiana (also called Pirates Den and Bayou), Arcade Ballroom, Showboat, Ding How, Kit-Mar Drum Bar, Dude Ranch and Club Esquire, as well as such nearby places as the Crossroads, Fat Boy, the above-mentioned Nightingale, Log Tavern, Dixie Pig, Hi-Hat, Tuchek's, Rustic Cabin, Potomac Boat Club, Capital Flight Club and Goose Creek Tavern.

Dances were held at the National Press Club, Wilson Line cruises on the Potomac, military service clubs at Fort Meade, Fort Meyer and Quantico, churches, lodges, temples, high school and college auditoriums, and nearby Maryland and Virginia beach spots. And there were many other taverns, roadhouses, and so-called beer joints where live music was performed.

When name bands came to town, they played the Fox (Capital), Earle (now Warner) and Howard theaters, or held sway at Uline Arena, Riverside Stadium and the Lincoln Colonnade. Some booked at Glen Echo and hotel supper clubs such as the Shoreham Terrace and the Roosevelt's Victory Room.

As elsewhere throughout America, swing and big bands caught on with a frenzy in the Washington area. Junior and senior high students and young adults listened to radio disc jockeys and late night remote broadcasts featuring such big bands as Tommy Dorsey, Jimmy Dorsey, Louis Armstrong, Bob Crosby, Benny Goodman, Artie Shaw, Jimmie Lunceford, Gene Krupa, Cab Calloway, Harry James, Larry Clinton, Glenn Miller, Count Basie, Chick Webb, Charlie Barnet, Duke Ellington, Sammy Kaye, Kay Kyser and Horace Heidt. Decca, Bluebird and Victor records sold like hotcakes.

When the big bands came in, hundreds of students skipped school to catch the opening morning stage shows. When the name bands were not around, kids went to Friday and Saturday night and Sunday afternoon dances performed by local bands. Many of them took up musical instruments and added to the increasing supply of local musicians.

The jobs in town were not all big band stuff. The groups ranged from trios and quartets up to thirteen pieces or even more, depending on what was needed. Whatever the size, most groups played versions of the big band hit tunes of the day. Musicians moved in and out of the various bands, and there was much raiding of players by the band leaders with promises of more prestigious and more frequent work.

Musicians were urged not to shake hands and introduce themselves on the bandstands because it would give the impression that the groups were not longstanding, well rehearsed units, which a lot of them were not. But well rehearsed or not, most of the groups congealed, and the musicians generally displayed drive and dedication and did a good job.

Money did not seem to be a major motivating factor. In fact, players would occasionally sit in with bands for the love of it. Four and five dollars a job were the going non-union pay levels per man. Union scale rates were more than twice as high, but many musicians remained non-union so as to work more frequently. By the end of the 1940s the pay was higher all around, but by then the swing craze and the big band days had virtually disappeared.

Beginning in the 1930s, swing enthusiasts and musicians developed their own language, such as "I'm hip," meaning *I know it;* "I dig it," for *I like it;* "That's cool," for *great;* "Don't hand me that jazz," for *don't lie or exaggerate;* "It brought me down," for *I didn't like it.* A "cat" was a person. A "hep-cat" was a devotee of swing. A "gig" was a band job." A "sparrow" was a girl singer. Musicians began to refer to their instruments, whatever the type, as "axes."

This was the scene that Fran Grady began contributing to when he picked up his "ax" to play professionally in 1930. Fran was born on September 28, 1914, in the Brookland section of northeast Washington, D.C. He attended St. Martin's School and Roosevelt High and graduated from Ben Franklin Business School.

He began learning alto sax in 1927 when he was thirteen years old. Although he took some private lessons, Fran was largely self-taught. The first band he joined was called the Rhythm Kings. He played alto sax, baritone sax, and clarinet. It was a five to seven-piece group that played local jobs and performed occasionally on radio stations WJSV and WOL during the period 1930–1932. Fran called this "our kid band," but in those days thought of it as "big time." He jobbed around town for a couple of years and in 1935 switched from alto to tenor saxophone after he heard Coleman Hawkins playing "It's the Talk of the Town" with the Fletcher Henderson band.

The story of how Fran Grady found his tenor sax is told in the following note from his files:

> *It was a bad, rainy night, and after playing a job, I stayed up all night so I could get to an 8 A.M. auction near the 14th St. Bridge and the Bluebird Club. I had an old Conn baritone sax in the rumble seat of my 1931 Chevy convertible. At the auction I spotted a tenor in excellent condition, way in the back under the counter.*
>
> *I waited for hours before the horn came up for sale. I didn't have a chance to buy it as all the bidding was done by pawn brokers, who bid higher than what I had (fifty dollars). I talked to the buyer after the auction and brought in my baritone, and after a long discussion, he took my fifty dollars and the baritone. I finally had my tenor. It was a 1933 Conn with a big bell. Was I happy! It was almost my twenty-first birthday in 1935.*

Fran played that same tenor saxophone for thirty-five years until he put it down for good in 1970.

The following is a list of Fran's activities and Washington bandleaders for whom he played during that thirty-five-year period:

Various club dates: 1936–1938

Joe Cochran: 1938–1939

The Trojans: 1939–early 1942

Wally Hughes: fall of 1942

Washie Bratcher: summer of 1942 and 1943–mid 1944

Paul Kain: 1944–mid 1946; early 1947-48

Fran led his own band at the Hamilton Hotel: June 1946-February 1947

Sammy Ferro: 1949-1952

Fran led his own band at the Cairo Hotel: 1952–1954

Joe Nardy: 1955–1956

Various club dates: 1957–1958

Chuck LoMedico: 1958–1959

Ira Sabin: 1960–1966

Sidney Seidenman: 1966–1967

Ira Sabin and Sammy Ferro; 1968-mid 1970

A list of all the places Fran played would take pages. Suffice it to say, he played everywhere in town and then some. Visiting name bands that employed Fran Grady include Charlie Spivak, Claude Thornhill and Charlie Barnet. During World War II, he made a V-Disc record with Claude Thornhill that included "Love Tales" and "Robin's Nest." V-Discs were made exclusively for U.S. servicemen and served as morale builders.

The Trojans band listed above was a cooperative group formed in 1933 that played the local country clubs, hotels, service clubs, and proms; it played for four summers at Colonial Beach for fifteen dollars per man a week, plus room and board. In a 1993 Kevin Wyrauch commemorative film about Glen Echo Park, Carmen Campagnoli, one of the Trojan's sax players, said that when he was a kid and first heard Fran Grady play, "He was like God," and when Fran joined the Trojans in 1939, "God came in and played with us." Grady, who was sitting next to Carmen on the film, displayed one of his typical contagious smiles.

The other Trojan alto sax player, Ray White, tells the story that when he was playing a job at the Jewish Community Center at 16th and Q, NW, Benny Goodman, in town for a theater date, walked in with a couple of his sidemen. Benny announced that he would be willing to play a tune, but had not brought his clarinet. Ray loaned Benny his clarinet and Benny proceeded to play "China Boy." There was a dead key on Ray's clarinet, and when Benny attempted to hit that note, nothing happened. He glanced at Ray White and gave him the famous fish stare known as the "Goodman ray," a look that reportedly had unnerved a number of Goodman's own players over the years.

I first met Fran Grady when I joined the Wally Hughes band as drummer in September 1942. I was seventeen and Fran was twenty-seven. The band played arrangements by Lonnie Wilfong plus a number of stocks purchased from the Campbell music store at 13th and G, NW. The Hughes band worked high school and college proms, country clubs, hotels, Club Louisiana and other spots around town. We had a "battle of the bands" with the Ray King band at the Washington Hotel lower ballroom. Our band was on the stage, and Ray King played from a bandstand along the wall. The place was jammed with dancers. To my knowledge, there was never a vote on who won the battle, but everyone had a good time. This was local Washington big band music at its best.

The Hughes band cut some recordings, including "The Man I Love," "Deep River" and "By the River Sainte Marie." Copies floated around town, and we received favorable comments from other local musicians. Wally Hughes stepped down as leader in early 1943, and most of the musicians, including Fran Grady, became members of the Washie Bratcher orchestra, playing at and doing local radio broadcasts from the Washington Hotel.

I did not go with that group, but instead joined the musicians union and began playing drums with the Jack Morton orchestras, mostly at the newly-built Statler Hotel at 16th and K, NW (now the Capital Hilton).

What were my impressions of Fran Grady during the Wally Hughes days? I was most thrilled to be in an outfit with the likes of Fran, who was already a well-established, well-liked tenor man, perhaps the best in town. Fran, playing in the fourth sax position, took the tenor solos with the band, demonstrating a broad, full tone. To me, his playing qualities were a combination of those of Ben Webster (of Duke Ellington fame) Coleman Hawkins (Fletcher Henderson) and Georgie Auld (Artie Shaw). Fran was known for searching and testing for good reeds for his mouthpiece to maintain his playing quality. On the stand and off, he was jovial, friendly and affable. He was well versed in all things pertaining to the big band and swing scene, an interest he maintained throughout his life.

Playing saxophone wasn't the only way Fran Grady earned his living. For thirty-six years he worked for the D.C. court system. He retired in December 1978 from his position as Branch Chief, Family Division, Superior Court of the District of Columbia. The following quote is from the announcement of Fran's retirement in *The Daily Washington Law Reporter* for December 28, 1978:

> *His departure will leave a void particularly for those with whom he has shared his vast knowledge and experience in operations and procedures of the court. His patience, graciousness, and keen wit in dispensing this assistance will be extremely difficult, if not impossible, to duplicate.*

Fran Grady's biggest fan was without a doubt his wife Lucille, who acquired enough memorabilia on her husband to fill a book, and I thank her for furnishing some of the information for this article. Lucille was a vocalist with a number of bands in the Washington area during the postwar years, including Sammy Nestico's. Nestico was former director of the U.S. Air Force Airmen of Note and arranger for Count Basie and Billy May. Other family fans of Fran Grady include his son Greg and three grandchildren: Olivia, Harrison and Blake.

When Fran passed away last year, tributes were forthcoming from many friends, including musicians who knew him from the good old days. One of the most poignant sentiments came from former drummer Ed Beavers, who wrote:

> *I worked with Fran about forty-four years ago . . . What a wonderful person he was, and he had to be one of the best tenor players in the country. I have always treasured the fact that I got to work with such a giant. I always wanted to go someplace where he was playing and just sit in the audience and listen to him. They don't make 'em like that anymore.*

Ah, those were the days, my friends. People had a good time with the music despite the late depression and early war conditions. But nothing lasts forever. After World War II, the swing craze and the big band rage started to go downhill as the vocalists and their backup groups took over the music scene. Some bands played on, of course, and people danced, but it wasn't the same and never will be.

Fran Grady's files contained an editorial from an unidentified Washington, D.C., newspaper entitled, "The Empty Bandstand." Apparently written in the mid-1960s, the piece lamented the demise of the big bands and the advent of the discotheque "featuring no band, no vocalist, nothing but four walls and a record player." Many music lovers lament the demise not only of the big bands and the swing era, but also of the past musical greats such as Francis J. Grady, who contributed in such a significant way to the long-ago good times. To paraphrase Jackie Gleason, "How sweet it was."

Addendum

The twenty big bands and their tunes that impressed me the most during the swing era were (band leaders in alphabetical order):

Charlie Barnet	Cherokee
Count Basie	One O'clock Jump
Bunny Berigan	I Can't Get Started
Will Bradley	Celery Stalks at Midnight
Cab Calloway	The Jumpin' Jive
Larry Clinton	In a Persian Market
Bob Crosby	South Rampart Street Parade
Jimmy Dorsey	Green Eyes
Tommy Dorsey	Song of India
Duke Ellington	Boy Meets Horn
Benny Goodman	Sing Sing Sing
Glen Gray	No Name Jive
Lionel Hampton	Flying Home
Woody Herman	Woodchopper's Ball
Harry James	I've Heard That Song Before
Gene Krupa	Drum Boogie
Jimmie Lunceford	Tain't What You Do
Glenn Miller	Song of the Volga Boatmen
Jan Savitt	720 in the Books
Artie Shaw	One Night Stand

Fran Grady in 1955.

Malcolm Lawrence in 1942 with the Wally Hughes band.

EPILOGUE

What a Life
by Malcolm Lawrence

The Great Depression and World War II
Were the years in which I grew.
Then marriage and my days of college,
Led me through the fields of knowledge.

For more than fifty years
Through laughter and some tears,
We've seen nine children edge through life
As they searched for joy and fought off strife.

No greater prize could be
Than to raise this family.
All have left the nest of course,
But frequently return to source.

Christmas, Thanksgiving and summer days
Beckon them home for wondrous stays.
With thirteen children of their own,
Our house becomes a honeycomb.

We the parents don't mind a bit
When home alone, we read and sit.
We know one day the phone will ring,
A sound that brings our hearts to sing.

(Reprinted from America at the Millennium: The Best Poems and Poets of the 20th Century, 2000, The International Library of Poetry, Owings Mills, Maryland. "What a Life" received the Editor's Choice Award for Outstanding Achievement in Poetry. Copyright by Malcolm Lawrence.)